RED EXPRESS

The Greatest Rail Journey — From The Berlin Wall To The Great Wall Of China

Text By Michael Cordell

Photographs By Peter Solness

SIMON & SCHUSTER
AUSTRALIA

RED EXPRESS
First published in Australasia in 1990 by
Simon & Schuster Australia
7 Grosvenor Place, Brookvale NSW 2100

A Paramount Communications Company
Sydney   London   Toronto   Tokyo   Singapore

Published in association with CAPTURED LIVE PRODUCTIONS PTY LTD

Project Director/Series Producer JOHN McLEAN

National Library of Australia
Cataloguing in Publication data

Cordell, Michael
Red express: the greatest rail journey, from the
Berlin Wall to the Great Wall of China

Includes index
ISBN 0 7318 0179 2

1. Velikaia Sibirskia magistral . 2. Railroad travel — Russian S.F.S.R. — Siberia. 3. Soviet Union
— Description and travel — 1970 — . 4. Siberia (R.S.F.S.R.) — Description and travel — 1981
— . I. Solness, Peter. II. Title.

915.704854

Designed by Jack Jagtenberg
Map by Greg Campbell Design
Typeset in Australia by Sun Photoset Pty Ltd, Brisbane
Produced by Mandarin Offset in Hong Kong

Jacket: In a country where the steam age still lives, one of China's many steam trains races through the frozen north.

Page 1: A traditional Russian dance, part of a festival on the Volga River.

Pages 2-3: As dramatic in repose as it is in motion, a Chinese steam train waits in a shunting yard in the north of the country.

Page 10: The telephones rarely seem to work in the Soviet Union. Russians joke that the Soviet Communications Minister died while waiting to get a call through.

FOREWORD

Our life is like one big train journey. The express train runs forward along the rails, rattling its wheels on the joints of days and weeks. It runs past the whistle-stops of Childhood and Youth, slows down at the stations of Maturity and Old Age, and then, there on the hazy horizon, one can already discern the sad, blinking lights of the Terminal . . .

As a child I was mad on trains. It was probably because I very seldom travelled. Every train journey for me was a feast and the time between them was full of anticipation. I was living in a huge dusty city in the Ukraine, with too many smoke-belching chimneys and too little greenery and trees. But there was a big railway terminal. Every day after school I used to go there with a friend. We would stand on a small wobbly bridge hanging above the tracks and gape at the moving trains below, watching them for hours on end, until our heads started spinning and we had the illusion that it was we who were moving, floating in the air above the trains.

Like most of my compatriots I was a typical armchair buccaneer. I collected train schedules and guide-books for my daily vicarious journeys, but was sure that I would never be able to see the world. Travel outside my country was the privilege of high-ranking bureaucrats.

I went abroad for the first time in 1988, when I was already thirty-four. I was invited to go to Britain and chose to travel by train. I couldn't believe that I had been allowed to go to the West.

My travel companions were a curious lot. We were all going abroad for the first time and our coach was a moving microcosm of Soviet life.

An awful thing happened when we were about to cross the Berlin Wall. The East German border guards appeared, leading snarling sheep dogs on leashes. They carried screwdrivers and portable ladders. After scrutinising us with their blank piercing eyes, they started unscrewing everything that could be unscrewed and opening everything that could be opened in the carriage. One of them lit up the insides of the toilet with his torch. They found nothing and all left but one, probably the most trusted, who stared out of the window as the train started moving slowly towards the Wall. Having made sure that no-one was hanging on by the rails, he jumped out. The darkness of night enveloped our train. Everyone was glued to the windows. Soon we saw the sea of lights on the other end of the Wall, the lights of the station called Freedom.

I always get carried away when I write about trains . . . Now you are in for a great train ride through crumbling walls and empires, through many epochs and time zones, through Time itself. The book that is lying in front of you is a big achievement. It ranks with the writings of Thor Heyerdahl, Jacques Cousteau and Bernard Grzimek. There are analogies with *The Great Railway Bazaar* by Paul Theroux, only here, apart from the text, you will find colourful and very expressive photographs which will make your journey as real as it can be. You will meet a mixture of people with whom you'll have an unhurried talk. You will be able to look into their eyes and souls. And believe me, you won't feel like armchair buccaneers . . .

Happy journey!

Vitali Vitaliev,
Melbourne 1990

(Vitali Vitaliev is the author of *Special Correspondent: Investigating in the Soviet Union* (1990). He was one of the first Soviet journalists to comment upon Russian life before Glasnost. Vitali has contributed to publications such as *The Guardian, Punch* and *The Observer*, and for two years he was the Moscow correspondent for the television show "Saturday Night Clive" with Clive James.)

CONTENTS

ARCTIC OCEAN

Tallinn
Leningrad
ESTONIA
Riga
LATVIA
Zagorsk
Kazan
Tyumen
LITHUANIA
Moscow
NORTH
SEA
BALTIC SEA
Gdansk
Vilnius
Berlin
POLAND
Wittenberg
Oswiecim
Warsaw
Leipzig
Krakow
GERMANY
CZECHOSLOVAKIA
Prague
Volga River
BLACK SEA
CASPIAN
SEA
MEDITERRANEAN SEA

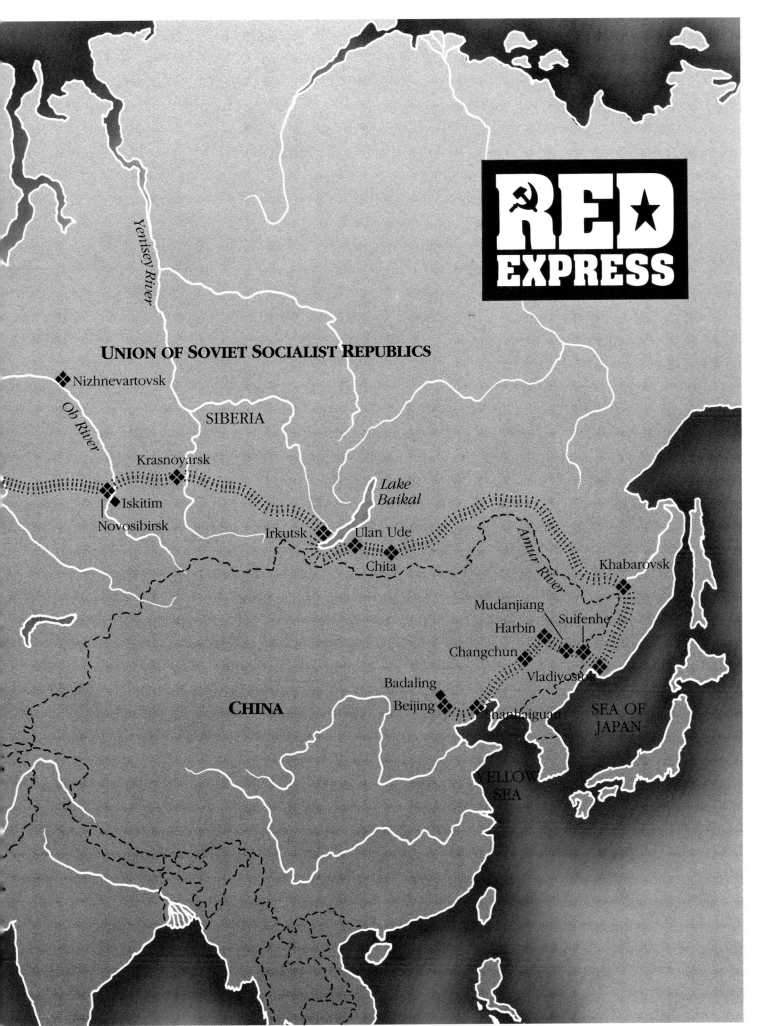

INTRODUCTION

As if this flesh which walls about our life
Were brass impregnable; and humoured
thus,
Comes at the last, and with a little pin,
Bores through his castle-wall, and
farewell king!

RICHARD III

As a child I vividly remember the moment, when crowded in front of a black and white television set, I watched Neil Armstrong set foot on the moon. I was in a schoolroom with the rest of my class, but even as children, we fell silent in awe, knowing we were witnessing one of the great moments of history.

Like billions of people around the world, I felt a similar, though much more emotional sense of awe, watching crowds of disbelieving Germans swarm over the Berlin Wall in November 1989. An edifice which had defined and divided the lives of a whole people, a symbol of the post-war division of the globe between East and West, was being wrenched down. The spectre of global nuclear war was fading before our eyes. Such moments are rare in history, but in 1989 and 1990 there were many, each of them a spectacular eruption in the greatest upheaval the communist world has seen.

Since my youth communist countries had always held a sense of menace. In their silence, I was told, they hatched sinister plans to expand their borders. Most of those fears were scaremongering, but the Eastern Bloc and Soviet Union always seemed as solid as the pyramids, an immovable part of the world order. To travel from the Berlin Wall to the Great Wall of China by train during such a turbulent period of change was an extraordinary experience I will never forget. As a railway adventure it was dramatic enough, skirting almost a third of the globe and taking in the famed Trans-Siberian, the longest single railway journey on earth. But beyond

that, it was a journey through one of the great epochs of modern history.

For the traveller these are not easy countries. I encountered much that was difficult and depressing, and for all the changes, too little joy. I expected there to be a sense of exuberance from Berlin to Vladivostok as people shed their shackles, but instead there was the trauma of uncertainty. To see the events through Western eyes is only to project our own sense of joy at the defeat of totalitarianism, but while we wax lyrical about the march of freedom, they despair about food and jobs.

It was impossible to leave behind all my ideological baggage, though I tried to keep an open mind. Too many people in the West have adopted the attitude of capitalist victor. Busy patting themselves on the back, they are blind to the problems in their own backyard. People forget there is some sadness too in the death of communism. As a means of organising society it had become corrupt, hypocritical and inefficient, yet behind the original communist idea was a vision of the human race that was essentially optimistic and idealistic, a vision of fairness and equality. That ideal was perverted, but there is a danger its most worthy values will be forgotten with the triumph of a system that too often rewards greed.

After 15,000 kilometres of travel through the troubled fortunes of the communist world I was left with two overwhelming impressions. The first was how desperate and inevitable was the need for change. Whatever your political colour, there was too much that offended basic human dignity. My second impression was of optimism and hope. What I saw proved that no wall is impregnable and no tyrant untouchable, that with conviction and solidarity people can rise up for a better world.

Michael Cordell
Sydney 1990

CHAPTER ONE

THE WALL DEPARTS AND SPRING RETURNS

Berlin to Prague

More than anything I remember their eyes, like young children's — wide and alert, darting from one sight to the next. The East German couple had just passed through the doors of Zoo Station in West Berlin and were taking their first steps in the Western world. They had come barely two kilometres, from Friedrich Strasse Station in the East, but they had never been so far in their lives. In any other city, the two railway stations would link one side of the city to the other. In Berlin, they linked two ideologies.

With a backpack slung over my shoulder, I was beginning my own journey through the world from which the couple came. It would begin symbolically as the train crossed over the Berlin Wall, and would end over 15,000 kilometres later at that other great edifice of history, the Great Wall of China.

No journey I had ever been on before stirred the same sense of excitement. Not only would it be one of the world's great rail adventures, taking in the legendary Trans-Siberian on the way, but it was also a journey through a social order completely alien to that in which I lived.

I was venturing into a section of a map, a region that had always been marked "Communist Bloc" in my youth, its huge mass dominating a large part of the classroom atlas. For all I had learnt about the land beyond the Iron Curtain — a huge catalogue of truths, half-truths, myths, distortions, and blatant lies — I realised I knew virtually nothing. Now the Communist Bloc was collapsing and

Once a symbol of oppression, now a symbol of hope, an East German border guard peers through what remains of the Berlin Wall.

12

what I would see before me was more than countries and cities, but the dying days of a failed social experiment.

Before catching the train to East Berlin, I stopped briefly to watch the East German couple's first few minutes in the West. As they waited to cross Hardenbergplatz, with their unmistakeable trademark of dowdy clothes and pale skin, they looked sideways at a West German couple wearing expensive fashions, and with coiffured hair and gleaming jewellery. I wondered if they felt any sense of injustice at the quirk of geographic fate which made one couple rich and the other poor. In front of them, a showy Porsche idled at the lights, while advertising screamed down from the sides of the buildings. The couple crossed the road to a fruit stall, stopping to stare at a pile of bananas. Just nearby, a sex shop beckoned with flashing red lights, ribald posters and vibrators in the window. "Solo striptease" and "Non-stop live sex" the signs read. They looked at each other, raised their eyebrows and walked on.

The East German couple had seen much of this on television, picking up broadcasts from West Berlin, but now it must have been like walking into a program on the screen. Zoo Station was a microcosm of the West, including a lot that was ugly; the brashness, materialism and the sleazy underside. Perhaps they weren't impressed, but now, at least, they had the freedom to travel here.

I pushed through a crowd of Poles dragging bags bursting with beer, soft drinks and electrical goods to sell back home, and squeezed onto the S-Bahn at Zoo Station, the train doors snapping shut behind me.

Within a minute the train had crossed the River Spree with the Reichstag, the former German parliament, coming into view. Burnt by the Nazis in 1933, and still

Seen through the windows of a former East German guard post, the S-Bahn from Zoo Station in West Berlin makes the short trip to Friedrich Strasse Station in the East. Most suburban trains link suburbs, in Berlin the train linked two ideologies. Crossing over the Berlin Wall marked the symbolic beginning of a journey which would end over 15,000 kilometres later at the Great Wall of China.

Left: *In the days before currency unification in July 1990, West Germans bought East German marks at a higher rate of exchange on the black market outside Zoo Station in West Berlin. Many West Germans were rumoured to have speculated on the currency unification by buying up East German marks in anticipation of a one-for-one exchange rate.* Top: *Still smiling after a long journey from Poland, these garden gnomes are part of the wide range of goods available at West Berlin's Polish markets. Many Poles make a handsome living selling Polish goods in West Berlin, then use the hard currency they earn to buy German products which they then sell back in Poland.* Above: *An island of Western consumerism in the midst of a communist world, West Berlin has long been anathema to the Eastern Bloc. Until the Wall came down, many East Germans weren't fully aware just how different their lives were from their West German brethren.*

Above: *Loaded with consumer goods so long denied them, two East Germans return from a shopping trip to West Berlin. Despite the low value of the now defunct East German mark, many East Germans had accumulated considerable savings due to the low cost of housing and subsidised food. There was little else to spend their money on.* **Right:** *The Berlin Wall looms behind the barren expanse of no-man's land, poisoned to slow the growth of vegetation. The Wall went up in 1961 to stem the flow of emigrants leaving for the West. When it came down in 1989, the flow continued as if the same people had been waiting on the other side.*

pockmarked with bullet holes and shrapnel from the war, I could see the first glimpses of the Berlin Wall just beyond it. I was approaching a site where two of the bleakest epochs of twentieth century history came together: the Second World War and the Cold War. Even in a country as far away as Australia, those two events had shaped my life, for my mother was a German refugee and my father met her as a Cold War soldier.

As the Wall came into view, muscling its way through what was once the grandest district of the old capital, I realised it was actually two walls, with the barren, poisoned zone of no-man's land in between. From the train, its thin, pre-fabricated concrete slabs looked surprisingly flimsy, but ever since the Berlin Wall went up in 1961 to stop the haemorrhage of emigrants to the West, it had successfully separated brothers and sisters, neighbourhoods, defining the limits and thoughts of a whole people. Up to a hundred people had died attempting to cross it. The last was Chris Geoffroy, shot in February 1989, and whose memorial I had seen covered in flowers beside the Reichstag. Ten months later he could have walked across untouched. "Honecker Diktatur" read a scribble on his cross.

Much of the Wall had come down after the tears and champagne of November 1989, but when I arrived, large sections were still being bulldozed aside with impatient enthusiasm. Tourists flocked to collect their piece of history. "You just don't understand what it means for Europeans to be able to go and take a bit of that Wall home," a Swede told me, but for the locals, the Wall was quickly receding into the past. German reunification was well advanced, soon there would be no borders between East and West. Checkpoint Charlie, the main crossing point, would be carted away, and underground railways rejoined. East

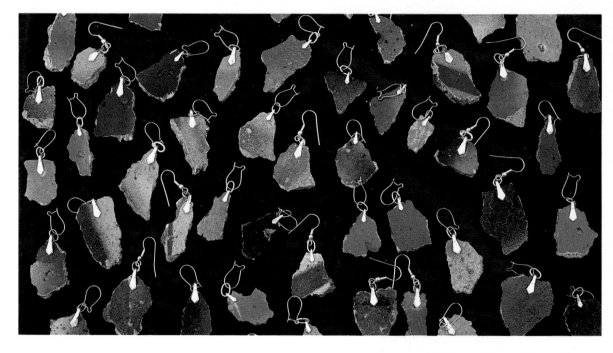

For his parents a fact of life, for him a part of history. Eight-year-old Brian Dieken of West Berlin chips off his own piece of the Berlin Wall while tourists swarm over fresh rubble as the Wall comes down near Alexanderplatz. Fully aware of its value, the East German government sold large slabs of the Wall to international buyers for much needed hard currency. From dividing a city to decorating an ear, Berlin's largest and most famous canvas will soon have completely disappeared.

German coins would be melted down for car parts.

But for the moment, the border remained, and as the train stopped at Friedrich Strasse Station, I headed down a maze of steps and corridors to the East German passport control, enacting a ritual that was in its dying days. A tall metal door clunked open ahead of me and as I walked inside the tiny booth it slammed shut as a border guard demanded my passport. In a few seconds he had stamped it, another door swung open, and I stepped into East Berlin.

As the crow flies, West Berlin was only a kilometre behind me, but it could have been on the other side of the world. The glitzy wealth around Zoo Station was gone, the colour had faded, the buildings were run-down, many still peppered with shrapnel as if the war had just ended. It was like stepping into the frame of an old black and white movie. The people in the street were pale, their teeth bad, their clothes drab. West Berliners unkindly described this as "the scurvy-faced East". The roads were full of Trabants and Wartburgs, tiny Noddy cars with lawn-mower engines, spitting and spluttering blue smoke as they darted by. A black Mercedes with West Berlin plates and tinted windows slunk by like a shark. As I watched the scene along the Unter den Linden, once Berlin's main avenue, before the Wall cut it short, I slowly became aware of how bad the air was. Sandstone churches and monuments were sooty black with pollution. It was like standing in a garage and I felt a dull ache in my head.

From Alexanderplatz, East Berlin's broad central square, I caught a crowded trolley bus to visit a film-maker whose name I had been given by a friend. Thomas's apartment was typical of many in East Berlin. The decaying building had seen grand days, but now paint peeled from the walls and every step on the dark wooden stairs creaked and groaned all the way to the third floor. As I stepped over a dismantled toilet on the landing, a serious man dressed in black opened the door. Full of the famous German angst, Thomas was one of many East Germans I met who were scared at the speed of reunification and its implications.

"I worry we will be like a Third World country to the West. We will just be a dumping ground," he said. "People have this naive faith in benevolent capitalism, but where once we depended on the laws of the state, now we depend on the laws of the market. Who will be thrown out of their jobs first — mothers with small children? The inefficient? We will see massive unemployment. The fear of losing jobs is going around. Who will buy East German goods?"

In his small studio, crowded with old video recorders and improvised equipment, he played me a videotape he had shot during the East German elections. While most of the media had concentrated on covering the elections in Berlin and Leipzig, Thomas filmed voters in a small village in the countryside called Ertsgeberger because "they are the grassroots, they represent the way most East Germans feel".

"We want to be German and we want to be free," said one farmer who had voted for the West German-backed Christian Democrats, the CDU. Another farmer in overalls had the following to say: "The Communist Party should never be allowed back in, they are worse than the Colombian drug rings. How dare they make any more promises to us? Only the silliest calves choose their own slaughter."

But what disturbed Thomas was a scene he filmed after the announcement of the CDU victory, when the crowd stood to attention and sang the national anthem. They nervously included the fourth verse, officially omitted since the demise of Hitler, "Deutschland, Deutschland above everything," they

Until the fall of the former East German government, the graffiti so well known on the Western side of the Wall was forbidden in the East. Making up for lost ground, a graffiti artist in East Berlin took the opportunity to make his feelings about Leonard Brezhnev and former East German leader Erich Honecker perfectly clear.

Top: *In a converted squat, young East Berliners let loose some of their pent-up energy. While West Berlin is well known for its vibrant youth culture due to the large numbers of West Germans living there to avoid conscription, East Berlin has an underground culture all of its own.* **Above:** *"People have a naive faith in benevolent capitalism," says film-maker Thomas Grimm, one of many East Germans scared at the speed of German re-unification and its implications. "Once we depended on the laws of the state, now we depend on the laws of the market."* **Right:** *At the East Berlin grave of playwright Bertolt Brecht, ugly memories of German anti-semitism are re-kindled. "Jews Out" reads the graffiti on the wall.*

sang. To Thomas it brought back all the fears of the Third Reich.

"This desire for unification can be easily transferred into nationalism. I have spoken to CDU people who refuse to recognise Poland's western border and want to annex Silesia. Megalomania has surfaced again." Just nearby the grave of Bertolt Brecht had been defaced with graffiti, rekindling another ugly memory. *"Juden Raus"* (Jews Out) it said.

Whomever I talked to, history and ideology hung like a yoke around their necks. For the Europeans, there was not the academic detachment of the classroom — history and ideology had torn their very souls. I never felt this more keenly than after meeting two Germans travelling on the train to Leipzig. They introduced themselves as Ute and Manfred, and I had first noticed them in the hall of Bahnhof Berlin-Lichtenberg, the main station in East Berlin. They had a young child, and while Ute nursed her, Manfred fussed as the train rolled through the grimy outskirts of East Berlin.

Both Ute and Manfred lived in West Berlin, having left East Germany three years before after a protracted battle to get permission. With their new baby, they were returning home to visit Ute's parents who still lived in a district near Karl Marx Stadt, not far from Leipzig. It would be a traumatic visit, and Ute was visibly tense. She had barely talked to her parents since leaving the East.

Ideologically and emotionally, the family had been riven apart. Ute's father was a founding member of the East German Communist Party in 1946. He had become a senior official at district level, just one step below the Politbureau, and remained a committed communist throughout his life. When Ute told him she was leaving East Germany to live in the West, he felt she was a class traitor.

JUDEN
RAUS

SAU
JUD

Bertolt Brecht

"It was the worst thing we could have told him," she said. "He broke down and started crying. It would have been better if I had said Manfred battered me. You could compare it with a staunch Catholic family whose daughter said she was changing religion. We were traitors to him. If someone had put a pistol in my father's hand and said 'your daughter is ideologically unsound', I'm not sure that he wouldn't have pulled the trigger and killed me. My parents threatened to kill themselves, to cut us out of their will. My mother vacillated — mother's love is strong — but my father treated me as if he had no daughter. It was psychological warfare. He was a fanatic, he had the same fanaticism of the fascists."

Ute had criticised the party while studying as a dentist in Leipzig, and life had become increasingly difficult. Not allowed to complete her final exams, her career effectively came to an end, and both she and Manfred faced growing harassment from the Stazi, the East German secret police. They later discovered that some of their best friends were Stazi informers.

"Most people who voiced a critical opinion were either sent West or to prison, or destroyed with forms of psychological terror," she said. "The Stazi were amazing. You can't imagine it as a foreigner. They knew everything about me. There was no personal future for us in East Germany. We had come to a dead-end. The most important thing for us was to have freedom."

On this return visit the tensions had reduced, but Ute's father was a broken man. "All the reasons we gave him for wanting to leave have come true. The Communist Party has collapsed. His life is in ruins."

I looked out of the train window at the dull green countryside, the sky an interminable grey veil which weighed down on land and spirit. The whole country seemed suffocated and beaten, and after Ute's story, I wondered about the millions of personal agonies that no-one would ever hear about.

We rattled by a small village and my eyes searched for people in the streets and backyards, but all I could see was a lone farmer leading a horse along a path; no colour, no children on the pot-holed streets, no sense of activity. Perhaps everyone was at school or work, but I couldn't help but compare it with villages I had seen in West Germany, picture-postcard places painted in bright colours, with flowers in window pots and a lively sense of daily commerce. The one splash of colour here was a bright blue CDU election poster that still hung on a telegraph pole. "We are one people" it read, "Quality of life for all". It was a clever slogan. When the Wall came down East Germans finally saw how different their lives really were.

Just two hours or so from East Berlin, I left Ute and Manfred at Wittenberg, the town made famous by Martin Luther as the birthplace of the Reformation in 1517. It was a ten-minute walk from the station to the market place, and as I got closer I felt like I was walking back in time to Dickensian London. The air was fouled with the acrid, sulphur smell of brown coal, and piles of it lay outside houses and buildings waiting to be shovelled into the cellars for heating. The cobblestone streets had a medieval charm, but in sections, gaping holes kept traffic at a snail's pace, motorbike riders in pudding bowl helmets gingerly skirting around them as if they were weaving through a minefield. It looked as though nothing had been built, painted, repaired or cleaned for half a century. At Wittenberg Castle I saw the door where Luther nailed his ninety-five theses, which began one of the most momentous era's in Europe's cultural history, and wondered at the irony that a city once famous for its forward thinking was now an archaic backwater.

Left above: The arrival of a new child and German re-unification bring happier times to Ute Stein and her parents in a district near Karl Marx Stadt, East Germany. With a staunch communist for a father, Ute's decision to leave East Germany and live with her husband in West Berlin tore her family apart. "My father treated me as if he had no daughter," she says. "We were class traitors to him." Left below: An East German train rattles along the line on the short trip from East Berlin to Leipzig. East Germany has sold high quality, locally built carriages throughout the communist world for decades.

Contributing to one of the most polluted environments in Eastern Europe, cooling towers are part of a massive power station at Espenhain, which belches fumes over nearby Leipzig. Life expectancy in Leipzig is six years below the national average, while at Espenhain itself, four out of five children develop chronic bronchitis or heart ailments by the age of seven.

With a serve of stodgy meat dumplings sitting in my stomach like a brick, I caught the train south to Leipzig that afternoon. Wittenberg had depressed me with its decay, and as the train travelled into the tumbledown outskirts of East Germany's second largest city, I could see my mood wasn't going to lift. Smoke stacks from a power station disfigured the skyline, their belching fumes hanging over the city in a yellow-brown cloud. The air was even worse than Wittenberg. The same smell of sulphur forced its way into the train and as I walked from Leipzig Hauptbahnhoff, it was like stepping into an ashtray. Armies of Trabants coughed past, many with their headlights on in the mid-afternoon to illuminate the haze. People winced at the smell and the city was caked in a sooty grime. I'd never had a stronger sense of a people being poisoned by the environment they had created.

East Germany has one of the highest per capita pollution levels of any industrialised nation in the world. By comparison with Japan, a highly polluted country itself, carbon dioxide levels are threefold, sulphur dioxide levels are thirty times higher, and dust emissions a hundred times higher. Some 2.5 million tons of sulphur pour from the country's power plants each year, the result of antiquated technology and poor quality brown coal. But the pollution does more than degrade the quality of life, it cripples and shortens it. Around Leipzig's blighted zone, life expectancy is six years below the national average.

Under the old regime, environmentalists were classed as dissidents and harassed by the Stazi. Now there was a fledgling green movement, and one of its founding members was Dr Helmut Reim, a friendly man with a grey beard, who lectured in anthropology at Leipzig's Karl Marx University. He showed me one of East Germany's worst environmental disasters, a major power

Above: *"I fear rising costs and the cost of sending my child to kindergarten," says Dorothea, a single mother living in Leipzig, when asked her thoughts about German re-unification. With the excitement of revolution over, many East Germans are concerned about losing jobs and coping with ever increasing prices.* **Right:** *Once persecuted as dissidents by the hardline government, East Germany's fledgling environmentalists are now free to campaign for a cleaner country. Standing by the huge brown coal pits at Espenhain is a newly founded environmental group from Leipzig. They complain not only about air pollution caused by the inefficient burning of brown coal, but also at the devastation caused as more and more of the country is gouged away by open-cut mines, destroying villages and forcing farmers off their land.*

plant and coal mine at Espenhain, just outside Leipzig. In this bleak town, encircled by smoke stacks, four out of five children develop chronic bronchitis or heart ailments by the age of seven, and just nearby, a huge open-cut coalmine gouges away at the very foundations of people's lives. Peasants are thrown off their land and entire villages destroyed as the mechanical claws of the coal shovels dig away at the earth. For kilometres, deep canyons of brown and black mud are all that's left of green pastures and villages. It was a bizarre form of cannibalism. The country was eating itself.

Beneath the grime, Leipzig remains a beautiful city, and I spent the next day walking through the narrow streets of the old town, flanked by Gothic and medieval buildings. Bach found Leipzig attractive enough to work here for most of his life and Goethe, who found the inspiration to create "Faust" here, described the city as "a little Paris". I visited St Nikolai Church, built in 1165, but in more recent times a gathering point during the 1989 demonstrations against the government. An eclectic crowd of people came streaming out of the doors. At first I thought it was a religious service, but I soon discovered that a senior member of the West German government had just addressed a meeting answering fears about reunification.

"We told him it has all happened too soon," a young man said, as he jumped on his bike to leave. "All the people who began the fight for a better form of government got pushed aside by this push for reunification. Now we will just become a poor cousin to West Germany."

"I'm generally positive," said Dorothea, a single mother with her child mounted on her back. "But I fear rising prices and the cost of sending my child to kindergarten. I study viola and people say eighty orchestras will go bankrupt in

East Germany because they won't have any more government support."

Outside the church a small band of protestors held placards demanding that one-time Stazi informers be identified in the new government. Over a hundred thousand informers were on the Stazi pay-roll, making it a force of repression far more powerful than the army. It operated from an imposing building just a few hundred metres from the old town centre and was officially referred to as the "Leipzig Insurance Company". Why they bothered giving it a false name I couldn't understand, because there was no other attempt to hide the building's function. It was a faceless modern building in the midst of medieval Leipzig, with radio antennae bristling on its roof, surveillance cameras at key locations, and a high wall topped with wire and floodlights around its perimeter. No-one in Leipzig was unaware of its function. It screamed of "Big Brother".

Ransacked by angry mobs in January 1990, I had no trouble walking through the building's gates and up to the front door. A poster outside read: "It's better to have fleas in your bed than the Stazi in government." And another: "We guarantee all conversations in the Stazi cafeteria will be overhead." There was wonderful irony in the fact the building was now being used as an employment office, because the entire Stazi had been sacked. As I walked through its maze of corridors, I shuddered to think of the physical and psychological terror it had housed. I wondered if the corridors of the KGB would ever be so open.

The East Germans had liberated themselves from the tyranny of a totalitarian regime, but they were still shackled by an inefficient economy. In Leipzig's market square, I watched a scene common to almost every town across East Germany. Traders from West Germany swarmed like bees to do business in the East, and they had descended on the square in force. One man sold chocolates from the back of a Mercedes, another sold bath mats from his BMW, and a semi-trailer was parked in the square selling poor quality hi-fi equipment. Curious East Germans flocked around each display, with the biggest crowds at a simple fruit stall, some people pointing at fruit they had never seen before. "What's this?" said a woman to her husband as she picked up a blood orange. He shrugged his shoulders. "I don't know."

"I can't afford anything," one woman told me. "But at least there is some colour now in the square. It used to be empty."

Nearby, a pair of smooth hucksters from West Germany had set up a small stand selling poor quality clothes at inflated prices and a second-hand computer which looked as useless as a penny farthing bicycle. Arrogant and patronising, they feigned to be doing a favour for their poor Eastern brethren, but in fact were swindling them. Here were the first signs of the new dumping ground which so many people feared. "You can sell anything you want here," said one of them in his spivvy shoes and chunky gold jewellery. "All you pay is three per cent tax."

Businessmen circled around Leipzig's five star Merkur Hotel like vultures over a dead cow. Mobile phones fused to their heads, all clad in identical dark suits, they snapped orders at bell boys and held earnest conversations over calculators. When they slipped into the air-conditioned luxury of their expensive cars and locked the doors, it seemed that Leipzig's foul air could never touch their noses, and the depressing poverty never register as anything more than a quaint anachronism.

It was easy for these rich West Germans to play the smug victor, lording it over a failed economy, but I wondered

In the centre of medieval Leipzig is one of the city's oldest buildings, St Nikolai Church, built in 1165. It found a very different use in 1989 as a focal point for many of the protests against the government.

In memory of a massacre: the outlines of bodies in Leipzig's central square mark the anniversary of an ill-fated uprising on the other side of the world, at Tienanmen Square. According to many people, a slaughter similar to that in Beijing was only narrowly avoided in East Germany when people took to the streets against the hardline government. Now fruitsellers from West Germany symbolise the slow transition to a market economy in a square once bereft of markets.

Plagued by pollution and decay, Leipzig gives the appearance of a city that hasn't been cared for in half a century. With derelict buildings tumbling down, the first wave of American advertising and its clean-cut symbols of youthfulness, seem a strange anachronism.

how well they remembered their history. It was East Germany that bore the brunt of reparations after the war, crippling the country's development. While West Germany received $US4 billion in Marshall Plan aid after the war, East Germany paid $US10 billion in war reparations to the Soviet Union. Whole factories and railway lines were dismantled and sent east.

The next day I met one of those rare people who are able to soar above the detail of daily life and look at the broad sweep of politics and history. Professor Markov was a retired historian, who had specialised in the French Revolution, and lived with his wife on the outskirts of Leipzig. A delightful, but frail old man, he blamed his poor health and dying garden on Leipzig's air, but his bright blue eyes were still remarkably alert. Professor Markov believed Eastern Europe was undergoing a long period of restoration, comparable to that after the French Revolution, but as a socialist, his most interesting ideas were on the very nature of the East German revolution.

"When the whole movement started it was a genuine struggle, intellectually and emotionally, for a better version of socialism. People wanted to do away with Stalinist institutions. But it went from a social revolution to a nationalistic one. This is natural in a divided country. For the simple German it was about reunification and the fight to win first place in the heart of Europe. For many it was a struggle for the Fourth Reich. The average German is even a bit proud there is a tacit re-evaluation of the past. Now no-one speaks of Hitler any more and they can announce again that they are proud to be German. This can become a danger. The problem with Germans is that you know where a revolution starts, but you don't know where it will end."

"For socialists it is a very difficult time. They are now obliged to go deeper into their philosophy and find out what the socialist ideal actually means. Politics is the process of transferring an ideal into reality, and this is where socialism went wrong. Socialism fell into the hands of an Asiatic despot after Lenin. This version of socialism will never come again."

"There's nothing wrong with socialism," said his wife, as I said good-bye to the Markovs at their front door. "The problem is man."

With twenty-six platforms Leipzig Hauptbahnhoff is the largest train terminal in Europe, something I soon cursed as I walked from one end to the other before finding the right office to buy a ticket to Prague. Later a shrill whistle blew under the station's cavernous glass canopy, and like a spider from its hole, the afternoon train to Prague crawled out under a web of electric wires.

I was knocking knees with a young, newly-wed Czech couple who sat quietly as the train left Leipzig. One of the great joys of train travel is watching people's masks slip over the length of a journey, and as time wore on the pair lost their formality and became as playful as two kittens. The young wife fiddled and adjusted her husband's clothes, and as she lay across his knees to sleep he gently tickled the lobe of her ear. It was an odd sensation sharing such intimacy with strangers, and I felt that rather than sitting on a train I was sitting in their lounge room.

On the outskirts of Leipzig I saw East German flags hanging from farmhouse windows, with the hammer and sickle cut from them. By now, the city had given way to hectares of private vegetable plots and blossoming fruit trees. A little further were open fields, with the occasional farmer tilling the soil ready for seeding. The countryside had the tired look of a land ploughed a million times over, with nothing wild or

On its way to Prague, a train leaves one of the twenty-six platforms in Leipzig Hauptbahnhoff, the largest train terminal in Europe.

natural to disturb its order. Rather than being inviting, it appeared desolate and empty giving me none of the comfort that rural scenes usually do.

We passed Dresden, on the River Elbe, and even from the train I could see the city still bore the scars of some of the heaviest bombing during the war. The train continued along the course of the Elbe, and by dusk we had dipped down into a steep valley and were winding along the river's banks. In my mind I had always imagined Czechoslovakia as a make-believe land of mist and medieval castles, and as we snaked up the river towards the Czech border, everything I saw confirmed that image. At the tops of steep cliffs, strange bulbous rocks were silhouetted against the sky like druids' heads, houses clung to the river banks below them, and the water, tinted crimson with the setting sun, was alive with mysterious swirls and eddies.

At Bad Schandau, the Czech border guards boarded the train and the East German electric locomotive was swapped for a Czech-made diesel. I was still revelling in the romantic musings of my entry into ancient Bohemia, but this soon came to an abrupt end when I walked down to the train's dining car for a meal. Six men sat at separate tables, rocking from side to side in listless boredom, staring at plates of half-eaten food. I had never seen a more dour collection of faces. A waiter sauntered up to me in a shirt that looked like a dish cloth, and told me tonight's menu was "egg". "What sort of egg?." I asked. "Egg," he replied. I ordered egg and beer and five minutes later a single fried egg appeared on my plate, accompanied by a piece of stale bread and a warm beer. No wonder the others looked so depressed.

It was past midnight when the train reached Prague, but in the short walk from the station to my raffish hotel facing Winceslas Square, I detected a mood far more buoyant than anything I'd

Above: *Snaking along the enchanted banks of the River Elbe, the train makes its way from East Germany towards Czechoslovakia. It is a half day journey from Leipzig to Prague.* **Left:** *Still bearing the scars of some of the heaviest bombing during the war, Dresden is on the main train line from Leipzig to Prague, where the ruins of the Frauenkirche (Church of Our Lady) are clearly visible.*

A fairytale city of castles and gold spires to which the violence of revolution seems a little alien, Prague is dominated by Prague Castle and St Vitus Cathedral. They sit on a hilltop in the Hradcany district above the Moldau River.

encountered in East Germany. It was a Friday night and the city was buzzing. Lively crowds streamed up and down Winceslas Square in smart clothes, and the air bubbled with conversation. Light and colour replaced the East German drabness, and there was a comforting hubbub of cars, horns and music. From the nightclub next to my hotel, couples swayed onto the street with broad grins and clumsy embraces. If this was what the old guard branded as Western decadence, then I was glad to be amongst it.

The Czechs were in a celebratory mood after their revolution. For months, Prague's fairytale streets had been cascading with an ebullience which had been missing since the Prague Spring of 1968, when Russia invaded Czechoslovakia. While the East Germans were preoccupied with the traumas of reunification, the Czechs seemed to be playing with their rediscovered freedom as if it were a new toy. In Winceslas Square, where two hundred thousand people shouted to the Communist Party chief Milos Jakes: "Milos, it's over," buskers were everywhere, performing with unabashed gusto to enthusiastic crowds. Czechs flocked to see the new uniforms of the palace guard at Prague Castle, while others queued to see *One Flew Over the Cuckoo's Nest,* the film made by Czech director, Milos Foreman, but long banned in his own country. Bookstores sold works that only a year before were miniaturised and smuggled into the country in cigarette packs. The plays of Czech President, Vaclav Havel, were all sold out. "We can't get enough," said a bookstore's manager.

Prague was undergoing the facelift of revolution. The former Czech/Soviet Friendship Society at the base of Winceslas Square was now the headquarters of Civic Forum. The Communist Party headquarters had become the Ministry of Transport. A

At the Skoda Engineering Works in Plzen, not far from Prague, electric locomotives have long been manufactured for use on railways throughout Eastern Bloc countries. Of the three hundred and fifty Type 82E locomotives made here each year, the USSR buys two hundred and fifty, many of which will be used on the Trans-Siberian railway.

Prague's city skyline remains much as it has for centuries. The city escaped major damage during the Second World War and despite lack of money, the communist government recognised Prague's invaluable cultural heritage, making some effort to restore the city's old buildings.

From dissident to President in a year, Vaclav Havel has become a world famous symbol of the Czechoslovakian revolution. A playwright who helped found the underground organisation Charter 77, and later, Civic Forum, he was one of many intellectuals who were instrumental in leading the protests against the government. Refusing to move to the luxury of Prague Castle, as was custom for Czech Presidents, he still lives in his old apartment.

giant statue of Stalin above the Moldau River had already disappeared during the Prague Spring, and now Lenin Street, Stalin Street and every other public place bearing a Soviet reference, was about to be renamed and depoliticised. Perhaps the most endearing break with tradition was the decision of Vaclav Havel to remain living in his apartment overlooking the river, rather than move, as was the custom of previous presidents, to the luxury and status of Prague Castle. There must be few places in the world where it is possible to walk up unannounced and knock on the front door of the nation's president. For years there was constant surveillance of Havel's apartment, now there is none.

It was hard to imagine revolutionary drama in Prague. With its gold-spired castles in Hradcany and the old town square, the tranquil city seemed as if it were set in the frame of a painting. The gentle, Turner light, gave the city a softness which violence didn't seem part of. In a small restaurant on Prague's outskirts, I met a balding man for whom the revolution had come too late. Jiri Bartonicek once worked for an import/export firm, but in the crackdown after 1968 was accused of being a spy by the security police (STB) after receiving friendly letters from international clients. He spent the rest of his working life in a foundry.

"It is not possible not to be angry," he said, looking into his beer. "The best years of my life are now gone. All I can hope is that Civic Forum will make things better for my grandchildren."

The new Prague Spring made me wonder at the excitement of the first one, twenty-one years before, which had set the country on a disastrous collision with the Soviet regime. When Czechoslovakia de-Stalinised like most communist states in the late-1950s and early-1960s, it did so with a taste for reform which went far beyond the bounds of Soviet tolerance. The appointment of the liberal-minded intellectual, Alexander Dubcek, as First Secretary of the Czechoslovakian Communist Party, coincided with a flowering of artistic and literary talent which screamed for truth and democracy in the face of lies and repression. The writer Jaroslav Seifert (later to win the Nobel Prize for Literature), and lyric poets Frantisek Halas and Vladimir Holan, were amongst dozens of major talents who inspired a mood of reform in Czech society. As Dubcek promised to take the state closer to the people, Leonard Brezhnev was aghast. The hammer fell and Prague was crushed. Dubcek became a forestry inspector. Intellectuals and artists who weren't jailed found themselves washing windows and cleaning toilets.

Russian tanks had rolled twice into Czechoslovakia, first to liberate it during the Second World War, then to suppress it. But in one of the great ironies of modern history, the tanks that crushed Prague in 1968 caught the seeds of reform in their steel tracks. The kernel of logic was carried back to the Soviet Union, where it lodged in the minds of Yuri Andropov, then Mikhail Gorbachev. Andropov had helped preside over the clamp-down in Prague yet, a decade later, he knew many of Dubcek's ideas were right. He had come to realise that Leninist planning did not work, that orthodox communism was intellectually bankrupt and that the economic gains of the West were growing every year. Prague has long had a significance in history well beyond its size. The intellectual basis of Gorbachev's reforms is not entirely Russian; it is Czechoslovakian.

On the day I was to leave Prague I visited two small, but faithfully tended memorials to Czechoslovakian courage. On Narodni Street, near the National Theatre, a set of metal hands reached out from a wall with the date 17.11.89 inscribed beneath and a candle flickering nearby. They commemorated one of the most violent incidents during the revolution, when police cordoned off a crowd of demonstrators and systematically beat them. And in Winceslas Square, surrounded by a low wall of wax from thousands of melted candles, was a photo of Jan Palach, the student who gave his life to the revolution, setting himself on fire in 1969 to protest on the anniversary of the Soviet invasion.

It was for laying flowers at Palach's memorial that Vaclav Havel was last arrested in 1989. Less than a year later the same man was speaking on national television as president when he was able to announce to Czechoslovakia: "Your government, my people, has returned to you."

47

In the company of Czechoslovakia's founding fathers, a tribute to Jan Palach sits in Winceslas Square, surrounded by flowers. Palach set himself on fire in 1969 to protest against the Soviet invasion of Czechoslovakia which crushed the Prague Spring the year before. It was for placing flowers at Palach's memorial that Vaclav Havel was last arrested in 1989.

With the Tatra Mountains in the background, a local train heads from the Polish/Czech border along the line to Krakow in Poland's south.

CHAPTER TWO

POPES AND PEASANTS

Krakow to Vilnius

The Polish border guards had only just stepped off the train when the young Pole lying opposite me made a simple comment before dropping off to sleep again.

"Poland has a problem with borders," he said matter of factly. "No-one respects them."

As the train left the border town of Karvina and clattered through the darkness towards Krakow in Poland's south, I realised the land beneath me had been invaded, reclaimed, and partitioned more often than a school-yard sandpit. Poland's tragedy is its geography. Fate has it sandwiched between world powers with few natural obstacles to invasion. To the west lies a sea of Germans, to the east an ocean of Russians. Tides of iron and steel, sabres and tanks, have swept back and forth across the country for centuries.

In 1772 Poland stretched from the Baltic almost to the Black Sea. A few years later the whole country ceased to exist when the division of Poland between Russia, Prussia and Austria wiped it off the map. It reappeared as a sovereign state after the First World War, only to be invaded shortly after by the Germans, then "liberated" by the Soviets. Finally, Poland's borders were wrenched 200 kilometres westward when Stalin annexed a sizeable chunk of eastern Poland and in return gave the Poles a smaller slice of prime German territory. More than simply redrawing borders, it involved the relocation of ten million people, causing massive social trauma. Lying in my bunk, an

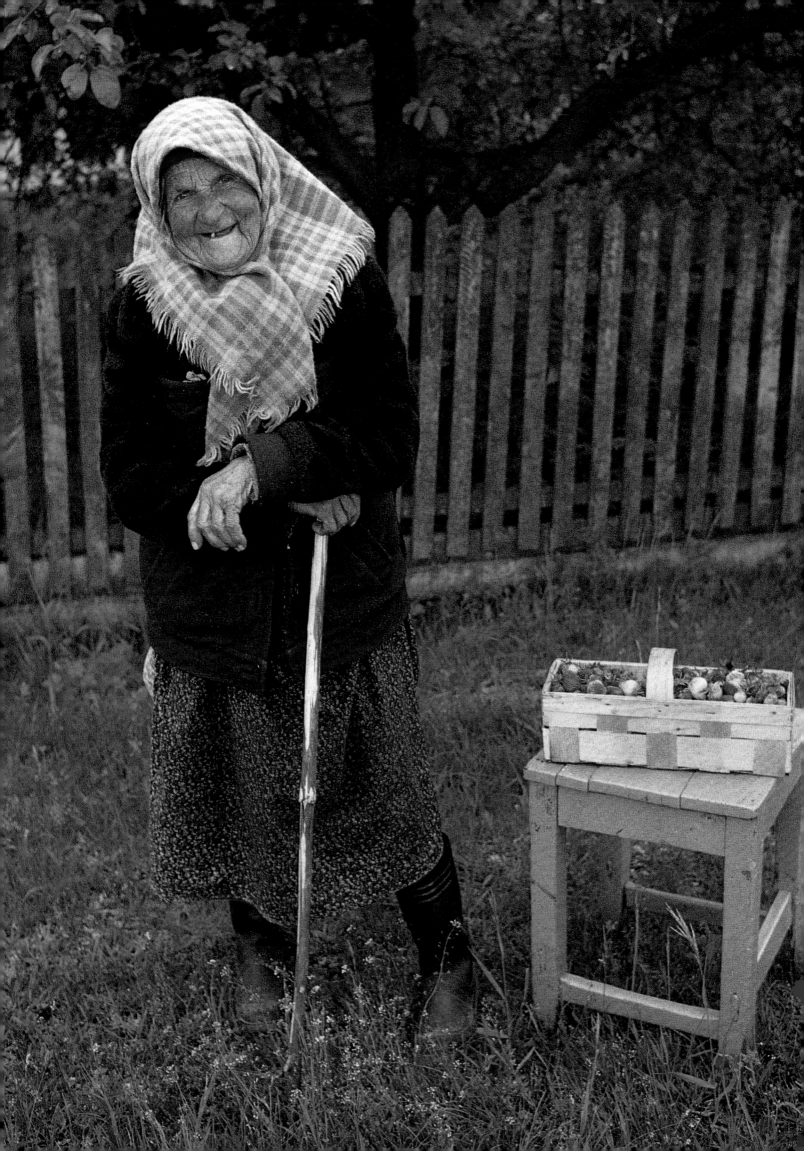

interminable squeak keeping me awake, it occurred to me that almost everything I knew about Poland involved death and ruin. That tragic history pervades the Polish psyche. Even Chopin's music was full of melancholy.

For all the anguish Poland has suffered, the morning view from the train window revealed a benign countryside looking as though nothing had disturbed it since the Middle Ages. Quiet villages with dirt roads and shingle-roofed houses nestled in shallow valleys, each blessed with a church spire, sometimes two. On the rolling hills with their patchwork of furrows and fallow fields, heavy-footed draughthorses dragged single shear ploughs and old wooden carts. Ponderously slow, with a bored air, the humble draughthorse still reigns in rural Poland. Tractors and harvesters are a rarity. It appeared an idyllic pastoral scene, a stage set for a period film, but it revealed the sad and archaic state of Polish agriculture. This was the legacy of the last tide to have swept across Poland, leaving an economic and political system which has shackled the country to poverty for forty-five years.

The attempt to collectivise agriculture says much about Poland's discomfort with the new ideology. In western Poland the vacant land of the former German territories presented a fine opportunity to begin collectivisation on the Soviet model, which would then spread to the rest of the country. But the resistance of the peasants was so strong that after a decade, barely ten per cent of Polish land was farmed by collectives. With Khrushchev's denunciation of Stalin's policies in 1956, the communist world floundered and the Polish government was left with no direction or will to reform agriculture. As a result, the system remained frozen where it was. Collectivisation failed, modernisation never happened. Most farmland remained under the private cultivation of

Above: *Horses remain a common sight in Poland where the draughthorse still rules over the tractor. Collectivisation never took hold during communist rule and modernisation did not happen. Most of the country's land remains in small, inefficient plots farmed by peasants.* **Left:** *At the age of eighty-seven, a peasant woman sells strawberries grown on her private plot near Krakow. Despite the backwardness of Polish agriculture, the slow introduction of a market economy in recent years has led to a greater variety and quantity of produce.*

peasants in small inefficient plots where they employed the same antiquated farming methods used by their grandparents. As I looked from the train at a man tilling a huge field with a single mattock, I wondered how Poland could ever hope to compete with the intensive farming of Western Europe.

It was a crisp, clear day outside, but when the train pulled into Krakow, my relief at escaping from the cramped and stuffy cabin was brief. In minutes I found myself jammed into a tiny Polish Fiat, knees scraping the bottom of my chin and the car's tiny engine buzzing like a mosquito at the back of my ear. The car belonged to a young man called Boguslaw who worked at the local television station and had offered to be my guide. "It's an old friend," he said, patting the dashboard affectionately as we stalled for a second time, then careered off on a tour around the city.

Boguslaw's dearest friend seemed to be Krakow itself, and as he took me from one sight to the next, he did so with the passionate enthusiasm of someone who loved his city rather than the rote ho-humness of the tour guide. Krakow was capital of Poland until 1596, before the capital was moved to Warsaw, but it still has the proud, medieval flavour of a royal city. "Krakow is still the capital of Poland," Boguslaw insisted, puffing his chest with civic pride. "It is no longer the administrative capital, but it is the capital of culture, science and art."

While Warsaw was razed by the Nazis during the war, Krakow remained almost untouched and it is permeated with history. The remnants of the city wall and moat still surround the old city, with its focus at Market Square, the largest medieval town square in Europe. The cobblestone streets running off the square reveal Baroque, Gothic and Renaissance churches at every turn. From the belfry of St Mary's an abrupt trumpet call sounds on the hour, recalling a thirteenth century trumpeter whose warning of the approaching hordes was cut short when a Mongol arrow pierced his throat. On the day we visited the square there was a blind gypsy playing violin at one end, a line of Russians selling gold rings at the other and a clutch of flower sellers in the middle.

"Now I shall take you to the heart of Krakow, perhaps it is even the heart of Poland," said Boguslaw, as we left the car and charged up a steep hill past a stream of religious novitiates in long black frocks. In a few minutes we were on the top of Wawel Hill, the site of the Royal Castle and cathedral, overlooking a meandering bend of the Wistla River. Built in the eleventh century, this place once sat at the centre of the Polish empire. Forty-one of Poland's forty-five kings are entombed in the cathedral, symbols of an era of power and glory which disappeared when the Polish Kingdom was partitioned between Austria, Russia and Prussia. The cathedral is also the resting place for Poland's most revered martyr, Saint Stanislaw, killed in 1079, and the first in a long line of Polish clergy who showed little fear of criticising authority. "Stanislaw damned the king for filling the castle with prostitutes," said Boguslaw, as we looked at the saint's ornate silver sarcophagus. "For saying this, he was beheaded where we stand. Then they chopped all his arms and legs off. It was very unpleasant."

Krakow is also Poland's intellectual heart, and just a few minutes from Market Square Boguslaw led me through a low doorway, its stone step worn into a smooth bowl by centuries of passing feet. It opened up into the Renaissance courtyard of Krakow's Jagiellonian University. After the bustle of the street outside suddenly there was a church-like quiet and dignity. Founded in 1364, the

Above: *Religion is never far away in Poland. Even at Krakow's Jagiellonian University Catholic icons are an important part of the architecture.* **Left:** *Former capital of Poland until 1596, Krakow still has the medieval flavour of a royal city. With its flower sellers in the foreground, the city's focus is Rynek Glowny, the largest medieval town square in Europe, dominated by the Renaissance Cloth Hall and town hall tower behind.*

Top: *From the the belfry of St Mary's Church in central Krakow, a lone trumpeter makes a symbolic call to national vigilance every hour.* Above: *The vast majority of Poles are practising Catholics, and from an early age religion is an integral part of a child's education. Dressed in white, these children outside Wawel Cathedral are taking part in a First Communion ceremony.* Right: *Descending from Krakow's spiritual heart, Wawel Cathedral on Wawel Hill, a group of nuns take part in the annual festival commemorating Saint Stanislaw, the Archbishop of Krakow, who was beheaded in 1079 for criticising the king.*

Top: *From the tyranny of martial law to burgeoning democracy in just a few years. In the streets of Krakow, Polish Prime Minister, Tadeusz Mazowiecki, a former academic, enjoys wide popularity. Mazowiecki came to power in 1989 following general elections which saw Solidarity take power in a landslide victory.* Above: *Politics and religion are never far apart in Poland. Watching the Saint Stanislaw festival, these women indicate the extraordinary patriotism to be found in Poland.* Left: *In the annual parade from Wawel Cathedral through Krakow's streets, clergy and dignitaries commemorate Archbishop Stanislaw, Poland's most revered martyr.*

university is one of Europe's oldest. Like Oxford, Krakow is a university town with some ten per cent of the population studying higher education. Here Copernicus came to the conclusion that the planets revolved around the sun, while more recent students have included Polish poet and Nobel Prize winner Czeslaw Milosz, and Karol Wojtyla, otherwise known as Pope John Paul II.

From the sanctity of the university Boguslaw drove me to the outskirts of Krakow in the direction of huge plumes of belching smoke. They came from the giant Lenin steel mill at Nowa Huta, and as we passed row after row of desolate apartment blocks that housed the mill's workers, I became more and more depressed. It is said that Stalin encouraged the construction of the mill so Krakow's free-thinking intelligentsia, who hadn't warmed to communism, would be outnumbered by less problematic workers. If anything, they strengthened each other against communism, but what the mill has done is cause major environmental problems. It was little different to what I had seen in Leipzig. Krakow's buildings are caked in black grime and respiratory illnesses are endemic. "The air is killing the city," said Boguslaw, turning up his nose at the acrid smell. "Everything is dirty. We call this the valley of death. There has been more damage done to Krakow in the last forty years than in the past six centuries."

A grimy worker outside the mill expressed the dilemma facing Poland's new government: "We realise how bad the pollution is, but we don't have the possibility to close the steel mill, or find other jobs. The only alternative is to make things better. We have no other choice. But this is expensive. Meanwhile we have to stay here and breathe the poisonous air as we did before."

Long before the Solidarity trade union was formed, the church was the main

Above: *A worker cleans off the corrosive dust that is destroying Krakow's medieval buildings. Suspicious of the city's intellectuals, it is said that Stalin ordered the construction of the massive Lenin steel mill at Nowa Huta so that workers would outnumber the intellectuals. The policy never worked, but the mill did succeed in polluting Krakow. Poland's environmental devastation is amongst the worst in Europe.*
Left: *Nicolaus Copernicus forever changed the way humans look at the world when he came to the conclusion the planets revolved around the sun, not the earth. In a university town long regarded as the intellectual centre of Poland, Copernicus is one of Krakow's most famous graduates, amongst many who studied at the Jagiellonian University.*

form of opposition in communist Poland, and one of its loudest voices was the Catholic weekly newspaper, *Tygodnik Powszechny*. Its concerns, however, spread far beyond religion. Read widely by non-Catholics and intellectuals, it was one of the few places where politics and social issues could be debated in Poland, albeit within limits. I visited the paper's office, just near the old town centre. It was a cramped couple of rooms up a rickety flight of wooden stairs, full of old typewriters and with not a computer to be seen. The paper's founder in 1945 is still its editor, seventy-seven-year-old Jerzy Turowicz, a dignified white-haired man with heavy eyebrows, whose desk was piled high with back issues of the paper. On the wall was a picture of Pope John Paul II. As a young priest of twenty-eight Karol Wojtyla had contributed articles to the paper and as Pope, has long been its protector and patron.

"The most difficult time was during the Stalin era when there was strong pressure and censorship," said Jerzy. "At the end of each week pages would be sent to the censorhip office in Krakow. On Monday we would be told by phone that maybe two or three articles would have to be taken out; sometimes there were as many as thirty interventions per issue. We weren't allowed to publish blank spaces, so no-one knew when something was censored. Then they controlled us by starving the paper of newsprint. When Stalin died in 1953 the authorities demanded we write about Stalin in a positive way, but we refused. We didn't much like this 'eminent statesman', so the paper was closed down for four years. We lived in a totalitarian regime where there was no space for free expression or activity. Now we can write what we like."

"I never believed this would have happened. I once hoped my grandchildren would live what we're living through now. Poland has had elections and while we are not totally democratic yet, we are stable. There are still communists in the ministry, we still have Jaruzelski, it's hard to replace these people after fifty years of totalitarian rule. There is no tradition of political maturity or independent thinking. But what we need now is radical and painful economic reform. There is no alternative. We need a different economy, but we can't change it from one day to the other. We can't build capitalism without capital. Many Polish people resent the reforms. But I hope they will endure them, not riot and strike."

The painful subject of reform was to crop up again and again with almost everyone I talked to in Poland, and never dispassionately. The whole country seemed to be shuddering with trauma and fear at the restructuring of its entire economic system. Subsidies and price controls had been slashed. Inflation, though reduced from nearly a thousand per cent a year, was still at crippling levels and some people predicted that unemployment might reach twenty per cent of the workforce after the closure of many industries and retrenchments in others. There was a growing cargo cult of people praying for the arrival of Western capital to save the country. Workers who had once gone on strike in support of Solidarity, were now striking against it, protesting about poor wages and rising prices. In Gdansk, Solidarity's birthplace, there were seven soup kitchens providing food for the burgeoning ranks of poor and hungry.

Nevertheless, Solidarity still had wide support, as a dockworker from Gdansk later told me. "All my free time I devote for Poland, for Solidarity. Because Solidarity did something good for Poland. We started the changes in other Eastern socialist countries. It started in Poland and reached Hungary, Czechoslovakia, Romania, now

In Gdansk, the birthplace of the trade union Solidarity, Piotr Gorniak goes on a hunger strike against the very union that brought the country political freedom. Alarmed at rising prices and looming unemployment, many workers are voicing protest at the hard cost of economic reforms in Poland. With added accusations of corruption amongst some Solidarity officials Gorniak engages in debate with the union's less critical supporters.

Lithuania. We've started this, this is something great."

Poland is now going through the agonies that most East European countries, and the Soviet Union, may also endure. Many believe it serves as a role model for the fledgling democracies and free markets of its neighbours, but the exact balance between socialism and capitalism is still undecided. The two great questions for Poland are whether Poles will be patient in their struggle with their greatest adversity since the war, and whether the entrepreneurs needed to create a market economy exist. As Lech Walesa, leader of Solidarity, pleaded one night on television to the people: "We are in the middle of a river. Is this the right moment to change course or come back? It is beyond doubt that the strikers are right. They are badly paid, nobody denies it. But at the moment when we are destroying the old system and making democracy, is it anybody's right to disturb us?"

Boguslaw's Fiat had a disturbing habit of stalling at railway crossings, but as we buzzed through the Polish countryside with these life-threatening interruptions, he seemed oblivious to any danger and kept chatting away about politics. "In Poland we gave the greatest opposition in the communist block. We never agreed with communism," he said, pulling on the starter lever another time as we sat perched in the middle of the tracks. "The opposition movement started in Poland. After the war we believed in the great future of the workers, but we didn't know the real face of communism. When we realised what Stalin was doing, it was too late. It was ten years after the war and there were Russian soldiers all over Poland." The Soviet presence was less obvious now, but even on some of the hilltops around us, were radars attached to Soviet military bases.

64

Above: *Playing for their dinner, a group of elderly musicians calling themselves "El Dorado," enliven the streets of Krakow. In a country that spawned as great a musician as Frederic Chopin, it's not surprising the Poles have a great love of music.* **Left:** *In the free market economy of the new Poland, anyone can open a shop, even in the boot of a car. Markets like this one in a Krakow carpark, have sprung up all over the country, providing a range of goods not seen in the country for decades.*

From the obscurity of being an unemployed electrician to leader of a revolution, Lech Walesa needs little introduction. With Poland's heady days of revolution over, the agonising task of reform is well under way. Speaking to the citizens of Gniew, near Gdansk, Walesa performs in his new, and sometimes uncomfortable role, as defender of the government's policies, not its critic.

We passed a market with farmers selling produce straight off the back of their carts and trucks: potatoes, cabbages and turnips. One farmer was butchering a cow's carcass in the open air. "Now there's more food, but it's more expensive," Boguslaw continued. "What we have in Poland now is Western world prices and Eastern block salaries. Food was subsidised, but people weren't paying enough to cover the cost of producing it. Bread was so cheap these farmers would buy it to feed their pigs."

Our destination was Oswiecim, a small industrial town 50 kilometres outside Krakow. To the West it is better known as Auschwitz, and it was the only place Boguslaw was unenthusiastic about taking me. We drove past lush fields with cows quietly grazing before we parked outside the museum, where Boguslaw chose to stay in the car. He had visited Auschwitz once as a school child, as most Polish children do, and never wanted to return. Over four million people were murdered at Auschwitz, up to sixty thousand in a single day when the gas chambers and ovens were working day and night. I felt a dull sickness as I walked through the camp gate just as millions had walked before me, never to return. "Work will make you free," lied the sign above them as they walked in, but the only freedom for most people was in death.

Poland has been described as a cemetery, a place of mass executions, wars, partitions and uprisings in which millions have died. Auschwitz was one of these places, but it was also different. It is a place of martyrdom, not just for the Poles, but for all nations who fought against fascism.

There was little talk amongst the many who had come to visit. A group of young Jewish children silently pulled weeds from the camp's perimeter. Flowers were hung over barbed wire which once buzzed with electricity. I thought I could

The world's most sinister railway line leads to Auschwitz and Birkenau concentration camps, near Krakow. More than four million people arrived on these lines between 1940 and 1945, their last journey before being systematically exterminated. In memory of the many Jewish people killed here, a group of young Jews carry the Star of David.

In a land of cemeteries and mass graves, Poland's grimmest memorial is the Auschwitz and Birkenau concentration camps, at Oswiecim near Krakow. More than four million people were sent to the camps between 1940 and 1945, arriving in cattle cars from all over Europe to face systematic extermination.

Flowers placed in memory of those killed at Auschwitz's notorious "wall of death".
While most people met their end in the gas chambers, an estimated twenty
thousand were lined up and executed against this wall after summary trials or
trying to escape. Most were shot in the back of the head, others chose to stand face
to face with their executioners.

learn little more about Auschwitz than I already knew, but seeing rooms full of human hair, glasses, children's clothes and the false legs and crutches of the infirm made me shudder. There is a big difference between knowing and seeing. The gallery of photos reminded me of those I had once seen at Tuol Sleng, Pol Pot's notorious prison and extermination camp in Cambodia. The condemned had the same expressions, of people who knew their fate. Some were defiant and proud, some were slumped and defeated, others had sheer horror in their eyes. My final memory was of seeing a small heart etched into the wall of a gas chamber. I understood why Boguslaw never wanted to return here.

The trainline between Krakow and Warsaw is one of the busiest in Poland, and the mood in my carriage for the three-hour journey was like that on a commuter train. Few people stretched out and unwound as they do on longer journeys, nor entered into the commitment of introductions and conversation. In the years of martial law, between 1981 and 1983, no-one was allowed to travel between Polish cities without official permission and trains were virtually empty. Now the train was full of students returning home for the weekend, and Poles going shopping in Warsaw.

As we nudged the outskirts of the city, a dreary procession of apartment blocks stretched for kilometres on either side of the tracks, a sight that would become depressingly common in the Soviet Union. It seemed unfair to criticise their ugliness here, as forty-five years ago all that stood in their place were fields of rubble. Few cities in the world have been more devastated by war than Poland's capital, and for the few days I spent there I couldn't help but compare it with the beauty and architectural history of Krakow, and come to the conclusion that

Above: *Almost completely destroyed during the Second World War, the remains of Warsaw's few original buildings are dominated by the city's more typical architecture: rows of drab apartment blocks which house the majority of the people.* **Left:** *In a country where the vast majority of the population are practising Roman Catholics, nuns are a common sight.*

Like a giant wedding cake, Stalin's gift to the rebuilding of
Warsaw was the Palace of Culture in the city centre. Identical
to Stalinist high-rises throughout the Soviet Union, it is
Warsaw's tallest landmark, standing as a constant reminder
of Soviet influence in Poland.

A Soviet and Polish soldier bonded in bronze represent a harmony rarely seen in real life. While Poles are grateful the Red Army liberated Poland from the Germans, they are resentful that Stalin chose not to intervene during the Warsaw Uprising which saw two hundred thousand Poles killed by the Nazis. The recent confirmation, long suspected, that fifteen thousand Polish officers were murdered by the Russians at the beginning of the war, has also soured relations.

Warsaw's soul had been forever damaged.

The war is still impossible to forget in Warsaw. At every turn there are reminders. Small plaques and crosses throughout the city mark the spots where thousands of Poles were gunned down during the Warsaw Uprising, one of the most brutal episodes of the Second World War. With the Russians pushing the Germans back through Poland after the Russian Front collapsed, the citizens of Warsaw rose up to liberate their city in August 1944, knowing the Red Army was only days away. But rather than help, Stalin not only held his forces on the far side of the Vistula River, he refused permission for Allied planes to land and re-supply the beleaguered Polish Home Army. Two hundred thousand Poles were killed in the fighting, many of them civilians slaughtered en masse by German SS troops. Almost a million people were deported. Then, on Hitler's orders, Warsaw was destroyed. In a vengeful, methodical exercise, the entire city was detonated and torched, street by street.

The Poles believe Stalin sat by and watched as the Warsaw underground was annihilated because the Home Army was anti-communist. Ironically, the Germans set the stage for a communist Poland by literally killing off the bulk of the non-communist resistance. The incident has long been a cause of simmering resentment towards the Russians, as was the massacre of 15,000 Polish officers at Katyn in the Ukraine, at the beginning of the war. The Soviet Union long blamed the Germans for the Katyn massacre, but finally admitted responsibility in 1990.

I met a young Polish woman called Biata, whose thoughts epitomised the ambivalence felt towards the Russians. She described to me a statue in Legnica, a small town close to the German border where there are many Soviet military bases. The statue was built by the Polish Communist Party and showed two soldiers, one Russian, one Polish, holding a child between them with the inscription underneath: "The people of Legnica give thanks to the brave Soviet army."

"You can't deny there is some truth in this, but there is irony," she told me. "It's typical of the propaganda of the old Polish Communist Party who tried desperately to convince Poles how much they owe to the Russians. When I look at that statue now I must say I am fed up. When I was a young schoolgirl I had so much of this propaganda put in my head about the friendship of the Soviets and the Poles, but then I learnt that the Soviet army waited for a long time to liberate Poland. They didn't help in the Warsaw Uprising. Now it's difficult to say who is the worse enemy, the Germans or the Russians."

One of the few things that did bind the aspirations of the Poles to the new Russophile government was the desire to rebuild Warsaw. The most remarkable achievement, and a testament to the Pole's resilience, was the complete reconstruction of the city's heart, the Old Town and Royal Way. From their very foundations to their red roofs and facades, the buildings were painstakingly copied from council records, photographs and the memories of residents. The medieval and Baroque character took decades to restore, and even now, the interior of the Royal Castle is still being rebuilt. Stalin's gift to the rebuilding of Warsaw was the Palace of Culture, which stands like a giant Gothic wedding cake in the middle of the city, monopolising all around it. It had less to do with culture and more to do with power. Like a flag stuck on a mountain top, it was a symbol of conquest.

But the building that most symbolised Poland's recent political history was what the Poles called the "Warsaw White House." An imposing white marble edifice ten stories high, it was the headquarters of the Communist Party and, not so long ago, was impossible to approach without stirring a hornet's nest of guards. Now it sits like a huge white elephant, largely deserted, waiting for a new life either as a bank or a library for Warsaw University. I walked unchallenged through its heavy metal doors into a large foyer, centred around a dramatic statue depicting the worker's struggle. A bored old man flicked through a magazine at his desk, barely raising his head when I walked in. I was here to meet Mr Bisztyga, one of the few Communist Party officials left in the building, and once personal assistant to Mieczwslaw Rakowski, the former Polish Prime Minister. After a call to his office, a man in his fifties strode out of the lift, his chest held out with curious arrogance.

"Welcome. I am Mr Bisztyga," he said, offering a firm handshake. "I believe you are writing a book. I notice that some people spend a few days in Poland and pretend to know enough to write books. Others spend years here and say they don't know enough to write anything."

I was taken aback by this blunt slap in the face but chose not to reply. We sat down in Mr Bisztyga's office with its portrait of Lenin on the wall, and he launched into an hour long, almost inpenetrable monologue — more like a lecture than a discussion.

"I am very pessimistic about the future of Poland," he said, starting to bang his fist on the chair. "There is no chance to rule this country on the basis of populist demands. I believe in democracy, but during the twentieth century we have changed our political and economic system six times, and none have succeeded. Our party said it would create a new approach but we failed. And now Solidarity is disintegrating too. The same will happen again. The problem is we never had a bourgeois revolution, we have not created a middle class. They are the guardians of democracy, not the

workers. The workers and peasants are only interested in short-sighted and populist concerns."

For a man who belonged to a party which was meant to champion the rights of the workers, he had surprising contempt for their intelligence. Now I knew what the "dictatorship of the proletariat" had come to mean. If this was what these people were like out of power, I shuddered to think what they were like in power.

I left Mr Bisztyga in his fallen citadel, my ears ringing with his constant raving. With the likes of him having run the country, I understood why the Poles had such a great need of popular heroes. Poland's old guard had so deserted the people's interests, the Poles found others to put their faith in like Lech Walesa and Father Jerzy Popieluszko. Less well-known than Walesa, Popieluszko was a priest who was murdered by the Polish secret police in 1984 because he so threatened the country's political order.

A friendly women called Sylvia had offered to take me to his grave, and as we buzzed across town in her tiny car, she told me that in the minds of most Poles, Popieluszko had already been elevated to a martyr. A large marble cross marked his grave in a neat garden beside St Stanislaw Kostka Church, and there was a steady stream of people paying respects. Popieluszko was a young parish priest, but in a working class area which took in a large steel mill, he had come to represent much more than a religious figurehead to his parishioners. Popieluszko's catchcry was "God, honour, homeland", and during communist rule and martial law his services were one of the few places where Polish patriotism and the desire for freedom could be expressed. His charismatic, pro-Solidarity sermons were so popular he had to address the huge crowds outside his church. In 1984, Popieluszko was pulled up by security

A tribute to Polish resilience, Warsaw's old town was reconstructed, brick by brick, from old photographs and the memories of residents. In an act of vengeful retribution, Hitler ordered that Warsaw be completely destroyed after the Warsaw Uprising. Street by street, the entire city was detonated and torched.

police while driving to Gdansk. He was beaten, tied-up and left to drown in a lake. Three men were charged for the crime, but many Poles believe the order for his murder came from the highest ranks of government.

Popieluszko is one in a long tradition of Polish clergy willing to speak their minds at whatever cost. St Stanislaw became a martyr for standing up against a king, Cardinal Wyszinski was jailed and tortured in the 1950s for standing up against a totalitarian regime and Popieluszko lost his life doing the same. Popieluszko's memorial, surrounded by plaques of tribute from Solidarity groups around the country, symbolised the curious union of politics, patriotism and religion which has been the soul and conscience of Poland throughout its history of oppression.

Perhaps the main reason why communism sat less easily in Poland than any other East European country, was that the majority of Poles were practising Roman Catholics. The Communist Party ruled on the hallowed principle that it exercised "the leading role in society", but in Poland the church has greater claim to that mantle. Poland's long history of oppression has forged the church's strength. Just as Catholicism gained in Northern Ireland when Ireland was ruled by Protestant England, so it gained in Poland when the country was ruled from Berlin or St Petersburg by Lutherans and Russian Orthodox. The Catholic church became the bastion of Polish patriotism, the protector of language and culture, and a formidable barrier to a new ideology. Add to that a Polish Pope and the church has probably never been stronger in Poland.

As we got into Sylvia's car to head back to town, I made a passing comment about the church's heroic role in Poland. "You know what," said Sylvia with surprising venom, "I hate the church!" It was if I had lanced an infected wound.

Poland is short of many things, but not churches. Arguably the most powerful institution in the country, the church has gained added strength as the focus of Polish patriotism during years of repression and the ascendancy of a Polish Pope. Some now argue the church is too busy building new churches while more and more of Poland's jobless go hungry.

Despite its unifying role, suddenly I was exposed to the age-old tensions that exist between the dogma of the church and the life of the people.

"People donate too much money to the church," said Sylvia, waving her hands about in anger. "We work for the church, but the church doesn't work for us. It does nothing for the poor. The church is like the Communist Party, no-one is elected. It's too strong. It was once the only possibility of opposition, but now all the church does is build new churches all over Poland. We don't have kindergartens, we don't have schools, we don't have apartments, we just have churches. You go to any village and it has three churches. Why? There is a joke that we need more churches because we need somewhere to pray for a new apartment! No-one questions the Pope because he's a Pole. Sure, he's done some good things, but he's very conservative. You know, the church refused to baptise my friend's child because the parents didn't get married in a church. And the church condemns abortion, then condemns single mothers! Sometimes I hate the church."

Back in my hotel I tuned into the BBC World Service to find out what was happening in Lithuania. I was booked on a train to Vilnius the following night but the latest news confirmed my growing doubts that I would be allowed in. It had barely been two weeks since Lithuania had defiantly declared its independence from the Soviet Union, and the tensions between Vilnius and Moscow looked set to boil over. There were daily reports of tanks in the streets, arrests, and key buildings being occupied by Interior Ministry troops. Some observers were predicting a vicious crackdown and the imposition of martial law. The BBC reported that the borders into Lithuania had now been closed to all but Lithuanians returning home. Foreign journalists had already been ordered to

leave the republic, but I'd hoped my innocuous tourist visa would let me slip through unnoticed. Getting into the troubled Baltic state might now be impossible.

I visited the Soviet embassy in Warsaw the next day and the enquiry room was packed with people trying to find out the border situation. It was like a football crowd, people jostling, yelling and remonstrating with the umpire, in this case a poker-faced Russian woman on the other side of a glass partition. Half an hour of shoving got me to the microphone in the glass, but I got my answer in one word. "Nyet!" No argument, no compromise, just "Nyet!"

Against all logic I found myself at Warsaw Station that night, waiting for the train to Vilnius. I had decided to risk the trip on the remote possibility I might somehow be allowed to slip across the border. Already excited about heading into the vast unknown of the Soviet Union, the added tension sent my pulse racing. Right on time, the dark green Soviet train slowly rolled into the station, its coal *samovars* (water heaters) sending out plumes of black smoke from each carriage. With its officious attendants, and the hammer and sickle emblazoned on the carriages, the train was an image of malevolence which stirred all the fears about the Soviet Union that I had been indoctrinated with as a child. As we edged from Warsaw Station and into the night, I thought of the great Polish writer, Joseph Conrad, and for a brief moment, I felt I was travelling into the heart of darkness.

Most passengers had obviously cancelled their tickets to Lithuania as the train was almost empty. Sitting in my empty compartment it occurred to me that the less I looked like a journalist, and the more like a regular back-packer, the better chance I had of being allowed across the border. For the next hour or

more I went through all my luggage and tried to remove anything incriminating. I ripped off the cover of a *Time* magazine showing an angry Lithuanian mob waving independence placards, and flushed it down the toilet. A clutch of newspaper clippings followed. I was loathe to consign my business cards marked "journalist" to a similar fate, but after trying to hide them behind the hot water system in the toilet, they too joined the long trail of rubbish I guiltily left behind me across Poland.

The train stopped at Grodno on the Soviet border. No-one appeared for an hour as we went through the bizarre routine of having the whole train hydraulically lifted off the ground while the bogies underneath were swapped over to match the wider gauge of Soviet railways, said to have been chosen as an obstacle against invasion. Finally, the Soviet immigration officers boarded the train and a gruff inspector yanked open the door to my compartment. "Russki?", he snapped. "Nyet", I replied. "Passport", he demanded, thrusting out his hand. I held my breath as he flicked through its pages, looked up at me, then back down to inspect the visa. Then, without the slightest hint of a problem, he stamped my passport, said thank you, and walked off. So much for a closed border I thought. Maybe the Soviet phone system was so bad these guards hadn't been told yet.

The morning came with a bright red dawn as the train headed north-east through flat fields covered in frost. The *provodnik* (attendant) brought me a glass of black Russian tea, and in the last hour before reaching Vilnius, I was still revelling in the fact I'd actually managed to get into the country. My guide would be Tomas, a young Lithuanian who had studied film-making in Australia for three years, and had just returned home. When I got off the train he bounded up to me, a cigarette hanging from his mouth and an

Above left: *A medieval vision from the train window in Poland's north. Visitors to the country often find themselves wondering if they are travelling through a different century.* **Below left:** *An unmistakeably Soviet train carries soldiers home after a term of service in Poland. With a new government in Poland and the reduction of Cold War tension, many Soviet soldiers are being withdrawn from the country, a retreat welcomed by most Poles.*

83

outstretched hand. "Welcome to free Lithuania," he said with a grin.

Like most Lithuanians, Tomas had a profound contempt for the Russian presence in his country, and everything he showed me in Vilnius seemed to reflect it. At Gedimino Square in the city centre, he pointed out St Stanislaus Cathedral, reconsecrated in 1989 after decades of indignity when it was used as a garage, then an art gallery. In 1950 Stalin's tanks had torn statues of saints from the cathedral's facade, and it still bore signs of damage and neglect. We walked past the KGB headquarters with a shadowy assortment of characters parked outside in their black Volgas. The building was only three storeys high, with another three floors below, but the joke goes it's the tallest building in Vilnius "because you can see Siberia from the top of it". At one time the joke wasn't so funny. Some 300,000 Lithuanians were deported to Siberia by Stalin in the 1940s during the Soviet takeover of the Baltic states.

Just across the road, in Lenin Square, we scrambled into the middle of a flower bed where, if you stood in exactly the right spot, you could line up the outstretched hand of Lenin with the cross of a church steeple in the background. It was a wonderfully irreverent image and, according to Tomas, just two years ago you could be arrested for taking a photo of it. I was surprised Lenin's statue even remained standing, for many Soviet icons had already been torn down in Vilnius. Lenin Prospect had become Gedimino Prospect in memory of the king who founded Vilnius in the fourteenth century. The street of the October Revolution now bore the date of Lithuania's independence, February 1918. On a wall nearby a splash of graffiti said, "Red Army go home!"

"The Russians say to us 'we are your liberators, not your occupiers,'" said

Above: *A Lithuanian at heart, but a Soviet citizen from birth, Tomas Donella is but one in a nation of people struggling for their independence. With a sense of humour about the economic and political system he was brought up in, he calls the Soviet Union, "the land of eternally green tomatoes". Left: With a wider gauge railway than the rest of Europe, crossing the border into the Soviet Union involves more than having your passport stamped. Hydraulic hoists lift the entire train off the bogies which are wheeled away and replaced with wider ones. It is said the Czars chose a different gauge track as an obstacle to invasion from the west.*

Tomas. "We say 'yes, you *are* our liberators, you liberated us from freedom.' "

Tomas had a well-developed sense of humour about the absurdities of life in the Soviet Union. He called it "the land of eternally green tomatoes", where nothing was ripe, nothing worked and no-one was happy. As we walked through Vilnius University, the oldest in the Soviet Union, he laughed at the memory of studying economics there to avoid military service. "It was like studying a science fiction course. But normally in any science if an experiment fails you abandon it. Here they kept it going for half a century. So we were taught one thing, but believed another."

In Poland I had found a plucky people who for centuries had fought against invaders and oppressors. The Lithuanians showed the same courage, but as a small and immeasurably weaker nation, I wondered how they could sustain their convictions. The tiny country's fight for independence had a chance for success, but in years past, people had given up on political struggle. To fight was futile, even suicidal. The energy of many young people was devoted, instead, to living for the money, and Tomas still seemed to embody that sense of recklessness.

Tomas smoked incessantly, as most men appeared to in the Soviet Union, and at the wheel of his father's precious Lada, he raced over the cobblestones of the old town and squealed around corners like Fangio. "No-one bothers wearing seat-belts," he laughed. "Here we don't care. In the West people are much more responsible for what they do."

In Australia, Tomas had struggled to feed himself by working illegally in a wrecking yard. "My friends don't understand the West. They have an idealistic view. All they see is the advertising, they think everything is easy. What we need here is unemployment

more than anything, just to make people understand that for every hundred roubles they have to work. Nothing comes for free."

Walking through the streets of Vilnius I had expected to see Soviet troops on every corner and military vehicles rumbling by in a show of strength. But Moscow's intimidation, for the moment at least, was far more subtle. The following day Tomas took me to the publishing house of Lithuania's renegade Communist Party, where *Lietuvos Rytas,* one of the main independence newspapers, was printed. The building had been occupied by Soviet Interior Ministry troops a week before, and a bizarre battle of bluff and nerve was still being fought inside. At the entrance was a small group of volunteers from Saijudis, the new independence movement, all wearing green arm bands and speaking by walkie-talkie to volunteers posted in other parts of the building. In the hallway behind them, observing all that went on, were groups of nervous soldiers. Most were pimply young boys probably terrified that the paper targets they had shot at till now may soon be replaced by the perfectly well-mannered Lithuanians they saw before them. Indeed, some even seemed embarrassed by their task.

The Saijudis volunteers escorted me to the editorial offices and, as they locked the door shutting off the troops outside, they welcomed me, as Tomas had done, to "free Lithuania".

"They be afraid of the new openness," said Maria Mudenieni, a motherly woman who had worked as a graphic artist on the newspaper for twenty-five years. She was a native Lithuanian, but amongst the volunteers guarding the newspaper were Poles and even Russians. "At first their purpose was to close our democratic newspaper and to start printing the newspaper of the Moscow Communist party," she went on. "But we

Conscripted to an army that subjugates their own country, it is one of the ironies of the Lithuanian independence struggle that these young Lithuanians may be ordered to fight against their own people. Resentful of this, a growing number of Lithuanians are deserting, causing alarm in the Soviet military.

have an order from our Lithuanian party to print our own newspaper, so we refused to do what the soldiers tell us. Their presence here is now a warning."

Rumours flew around the office as they did across Vilnius. Paratroopers with automatic weapons were waiting in the basement. Troops were about to take over the television station. Landsbergis would be jailed. The United States had made a deal with Gorbachev to "swap" an attack on Cuba for an attack on Lithuania. No-one knew what to expect.

"I asked one soldier if he would shoot me," said a volunteer. "He was Ukrainian and he told me he would never use a gun. We have no strength, only moral strength. These are our only weapons: moral strength and calmness."

The greatest show of Lithuania's determination was to come that afternoon when almost half the good citizens of Vilnius, a staggering 300,000 people, attended a rally to reassert their independence. The streets were jammed for kilometres leading to the demonstration, electric trolley buses bursting with people, youngsters waving the Lithuanian flag from car windows. The rally had a defiant but festive air, with children on shoulders and fingers held in victory signs. The shotgun marriage with the Soviet Union was over they had come to say. All that remained were the terms of the settlement. But just as the independence leader, Vytautas Landsbergis began to speak, an ominous drone could be heard. Every head in the crowd turned as a Soviet military helicopter loomed barely 30 metres above, drowning the speeches. Fists rose up in the air as a small door opened at the rear of the helicopter and thousands of propaganda leaflets started spilling down onto the crowd.

"Look at them," yelled Landsbergis above the racket. "They have garbaged the world for seventy years and still they do it. This day we declared

independence will be the day that marked the beginning of the end of the Russian empire."

An old woman standing beside me shook her fist in the air and chanted "shame, shame, shame" with the crowd. Then she turned to me, silver teeth in an otherwise empty mouth. "They're trying to frighten us," she said, "but they don't understand that Lithuanians don't fear to die."

The scene symbolised for me the wave of uprisings against Soviet control and totalitarian rule that had just swept the communist world, not only in Lithuania, but throughout Eastern Europe. As I travelled briefly through Latvia and Estonia, Baltic states also demanding their independence, the image of that old woman stayed with me. It was an image of moral strength against physical might and arrogance. Eastern Europe had shown that moral strength will eventually triumph.

Top left: *Proudly wearing the Lithuanian colours, this Vilnius resident can remember the golden era of Lithuanian independence before the Soviets invaded the country in 1940. Granted nationhood in 1918, the Lithuanians regarded themselves on a par with Scandinavian countries on the other side of the Baltic before their country was swallowed up by the Soviet empire.*
Bottom left: *As in Poland, the Lithuanian sense of national identity is closely linked with religion. This wooden carving was carried across the country in a display of religious and patriotic fervour.*

CHAPTER THREE

INTO THE HEART OF MOTHER RUSSIA

Leningrad to Moscow

I first noticed her as the train crawled arthritically out of Tallinn Station on the four-hour trip to Leningrad. She was in her seventies, a stocky and robust Russian woman wearing a scarf on her head and a businesslike pair of gumboots. Her ageing daughter stood on the platform and as the train departed they put their fingers to the window in a touching goodbye.

She appeared to match that famous Russian stereotype . . . the *babushka,* or grandmother. It's the babushkas who have shouldered many of the vast agonies the Russian people have lived under since the revolution. Some lost their husbands to the war, others to Stalin's terror, but for much of their lives they have waged a daily battle just to feed their families. If courage and perseverance are a measure of greatness, then it isn't the cold war generals and cosmonauts who deserve to be the official heroes of Soviet society, but the humble babushkas. The woman with the tired, kind face sitting opposite me was no exception.

As the train made its sluggish way over fields clogged with water after the winter thaw, I discovered she had lived in Leningrad all her life. With a slow sadness in which the pauses said more than the words, she told me about Leningrad's greatest horror . . . the nine hundred days the Germans held the city under siege during the Second World War. Over a million people died, the vast majority from cold and starvation, not

A little private enterprise such as selling flowers near a railway station, can be a babushka's source of livelihood. The flowers have probably been grown on a small plot of land in a village, or on the outskirts of the city. Life is tougher in the country, with supplies scarce, but you can cultivate a garden.

91

bombs. On the worst days, in the depths of winter, with no electricity or heating, thousands of people died each day. Familes ate their pets. Some caught rats, and others made soup from carpenter's glue. There were also reports of cannibalism. In the space of just ten days during the siege the babushka told me she lost her mother, her husband and a daughter. As a nurse, she treated thousands of people who had simply dropped in the streets from hunger. No family was unaffected. Like all Russians, history weighed heavily upon her. The trauma the Soviet Union went through during the "Great Fatherland War" goes a long way to explaining the country's preoccupation with defence.

"You can read all this in a book," she said to me as we nudged the outskirts of Leningrad. "But it is not the full truth. It is impossible to explain to anyone what it was like, how bad it was."

On a sunny spring day in Leningrad it takes a special effort of will to imagine such horrors, for the city's charms can be overpowering. The sun reflects giddily off the River Neva and lining its embankments are the pastel coloured palaces and official buildings which help give the city its grand elegance. On a small beach bordering the St Peter and Paul Fortress you can lazily drink in the sun as white bodies bounce past in bikinis and G-strings, while others stroll by still bound in furs and scarves against the crisp breeze. It's a playground for simple pleasures; lovers swapping gentle kisses, parents pushing prams, excited children playing hide-and-seek on battlements that have seen revolution and war.

When the St Peter and Paul Fortress was begun in 1703 on the Baltic beachhead the Russians had seized from the Swedes, it marked the beginning of one of the great obsessions in history. Abhorred by the isolation of his country after centuries of Tatar domination, Peter

the Great set about shaking Russia from its medieval slumber, dragging it by the ear towards Europe and the modern world.

Replacing Moscow as the new Russian capital, the city first known as St Petersburg symbolised everything the impassioned Czar aspired to. With its proximity to Europe, St Petersburg opened a window to the West that Russia had never had. European architects and craftsmen were employed to create a city of eighteenth century refinement. Bathed in its soft northern light, the result was something which made more reference to Venice and Amsterdam than to Moscow and Russia's own Byzantine history.

Over two metres tall, with a physical presence to match his ambitions, Peter tried to rid Russia of its boorishness with a broad sweep of his hand. No matter that thousands died driving piles into the marshy islands to create the city's foundations, to Peter the cost was small. Dowdy Russian wives were thrust into petite French fashions. Off went the beards of the nobility and their ankle-length caftans, in favour of Western dress. Even speaking French became *de rigeur.*

The obsession with things Western continued long after Peter died in 1725, with the most spectacular display in the Hermitage Museum of the Winter Palace. It houses art not only collected by the Czars, but works appropriated from wealthy Russian merchants after the revolution. As a tribute to the best of European art, there are few collections that better it, despite the fact that some of the best works were sold off to raise hard currency in the early 1930s. Many great artists are represented here, from da Vinci, to Michelangelo, Rembrandt, Rubens, van Gogh and the modern masters.

But for all Peter the Great's tinkering with the facade of Russian life, one senses that his efforts never went more than

Basking outside Leningrad's historic St Peter and Paul Fortress, bathers take in the sun before the onset of a long winter. The fortress was the first stone construction in St Petersburg, begun in 1703, and symbolised Peter the Great's grand vision of the city as a door to the West, leading Russia into the modern world.

93

Above: *The Kunstkammer Museum and the St Peter and Paul Cathedral with its 122 metre gilded spire. Peter the Great is buried under the cathedral in a vault, as are all the Czars who followed him. All that is, but the last of the Romanovs, Nicholas II, who was shot dead with his family after the Revolution. He was denied the honour.* **Right:** *The Main Staircase of Leningrad's State Hermitage Museum in the Czar's Winter Palace. The Baroque splendour of the staircase is the work of Italian architect Rastrelli, but it underwent some changes after fire damaged a section of the palace in 1837. Each year up to three million people climb the staircase to see how the Czars lived and to view one of the world's great art collections in the Hermitage Gallery.*

skin deep. For while St Petersburg and western Russia may have taken on some of the trappings of Europe, the vast empire stretching thousands of kilometres to the east remained largely unchanged. Such self-conscious mimicry of the West spoke of a national inferiority complex, which still exists today in a different form. Gorbachev, in his own way, is struggling to achieve what Peter the Great attempted to. Both are reformers, heaving their country into a new age. The abject failure of the Soviet system to fully deliver its people into the twentieth century has meant the window to the West is once again open, after decades of being firmly closed.

I found a few hours walking the streets soon tempers the city's romanticism. For while Leningrad shares the problems of every Soviet city, its mood seems sadder, and it is suffused with the lost glory of a former capital, an insult made worse because the city is literally falling apart. Seen at close quarters, much of Leningrad is in an advanced state of decay. Cars stop abruptly in mid-flight to dodge potholes in the street, trams rattle and shake over lines that sink ominously into the bitumen and much of the wonderful detail which adorns the Russian Baroque buildings has dropped off. A face carved in sandstone becomes barely discernible after years of being attacked by a cancerous neglect. In the age of *glasnost,* newspapers run regular features on the problem. "The cradle of the revolution — or the former capital of the former Russian Empire — is dying," cries *Moscow News* at the start of a scathing attack.

In Leningrad's bleak back alleys, the despairing spirit of Dostoevsky's novels still lives on. There's little trouble finding characters racked with anguish and turmoil here. The most visible are the city's punks. While the punk movement in the West has largely been rendered

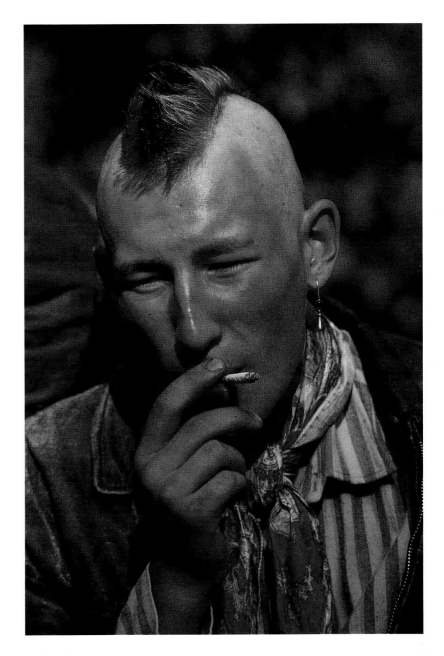

Left: *Leningrad is suffused with the lost glory of a former capital. Most of its buildings are a melancholy grey, victims of disrepair and neglect in a country that can't afford to maintain them. Combined with the city's notoriously grey skies, it can create a sombre mood.* **Above:** *Known as Nikolai to his parents and "Rat" to his friends, this Leningrad punk is making a clear statement about the state of his nation. Many Soviet youths feel cheated; cheated of a decent future and cheated by the system. "They lied, they're lying, and they will still lie to us," he says. "Those at the top still have much more than the working class."*

meaningless since it was hijacked by the fashion industry, here it can claim a real legitimacy. In the grotty courtyard of a decrepit apartment block teenagers "Dog", "Rat" and "Chuk", as they called themselves, displayed a cynicism born from total disenchantment.

"To put it politely, there's no life here at all," said Dog. "It's just a hole, that's all."

Their three mohawks nodded in agreement.

"I think our grandparents lived better," pitched in Dog's girlfriend, Chuk, "because we can't buy stuff cheaply like they could. Now sugar, tea, soap, flour, everything's rationed; a certain amount per month. I sit now and think, what will my children have? And I feel very sad."

"The Soviet people used to be the happiest people in the world because they didn't know how badly they lived," laughed Rat. "The leadership lied, they're lying, and they will still lie to us. Those at the top have much more than the working class. So in our way of life the most important thing is vegetating, denying everything. We do what we want."

In the midst of this despair and decay lives Nikita Tolstoy. His apartment block overlooks one of Leningrad's countless treacle-brown canals, a short distance from the city centre. He is one of the country's most respected scientists, but lives in a building which would come close to being condemned in the West. The concrete stairs are crumbling and when your eyes adjust to the half-light of the foyer, you see the small piles of dirt that have collected in the corners. Cobwebs hold together the last chips of battle-green paint on the walls and the lift which takes you to the top floor doesn't look safe enough to be a dumb-waiter. By comparison to some, however, he and his wife live well. They have a Volga in the driveway, be it twenty years old, and his position has allowed him

Tracing family links to the great Russian writer, Leo Tolstoy, Nikita Tolstoy is a physicist. He would now be a Count had it not been for the revolution of 1917. With Soviet history long at the mercy of political expediency, Nikita is a living reminder of what has happened to Russian nobility and the intelligentsia.

much travel. But any grimness shrank away as the door opened. The warm hand of a big man extended to greet me, along with the wafting smells of a busy kitchen.

"I know what you're thinking," he said, leading me into his lounge with its decrepit parquet floor and rickety chairs, "but we are comfortable."

Nikita traces his roots back to Peter Andryeovich Tolstoy, a friend and collaborator of Peter the Great. It is Peter Andryeovich's son who provides the distant link Nikita shares with the great Russian writer, Leo Tolstoy. Descendant himself from Russian nobility, Nikita was born in 1917 and would be a count had it not been for the revolution of that year. It's a loss he doesn't mourn.

"Well, what do you think of my country?" he suddenly asked, sweeping back a few tenuous wisps of white hair over his head.

It was one of those awkward questions you squirm over unless you've got something positive to say. Rather than lie, or gush about Leningrad's beauty, I said that as an outsider, I found myself deeply shocked. I couldn't help but feel an overwhelming sense of tragedy at what the Russian people had been through. But I couldn't understand that given the country's history and its on-going poverty, why there wasn't massive anger among the people.

"You have heard of Pavlov's experiments?" he asked. "Well there are many parallels in my country. Pavlov took a dog and beat it every day at twelve o'clock. For the first few days the dog was hysterical, barking and foaming at the mouth every time it was beaten. After two weeks the dog stood quietly while it was hit, just shuddering and trembling. Before long it began to lick the hand of its tormentor after every beating. Similar things happen to people with oversuffering. In the past, people here learnt that to resist only made

things worse. Our oversuffering has produced this kind of nightmarish quietness, a social stupor that's stopped any reaction to the terrible path of events."

The man who beat the Soviet people harder than anyone else was, of course, Joseph Stalin. As a member of the intelligentsia, Nikita moved in a circle of people decimated by Stalin's purges.

"There was selective extermination during Stalin's time of people who had a free mind and free speech. It was like a big mowing machine that cut off everything that popped up above the level of the grass. Just a free judgment on something made you suspect. No one could have ideas that didn't belong to the set of unified ideas laid down by directives from above."

"We survived by belonging to a trade union," he continued, stubbing his cigarette in a growing pile on the saucer of his tea-cup. "It was a trade union of decency. During Stalin's time there was this curious phenomenon where certain groups of people became united by the terror and developed a complete confidence in each other's decency. You could only have normal social and professional relationships with these people, because you were sure you wouldn't be denounced, deported or shot by being honest. You developed an acute sense of evaluating someone's personality. You couldn't make a mistake or you were automatically eliminated from this side of the barbed wire."

Nikita felt the fear of the Stalin era, but instead of licking his master's hand, he made jokes behind his back. Humour sustained many people during the dark ages of repression, as it does now. He pointed to a small broken window behind me and laughed. "See that window? It's been broken since 1963! Glass is impossible to get. I can't even get windscreen wipers for my car unless I buy them on the black market!"

What I found most inspiring about this compassionate, intelligent man, in his black darned skivvy, was his enduring optimism. For despite a history that stole his friends and a system that assaults his dignity, his spirit rises above it. In others, it has been crushed. It seemed many people were impressed by Nikita, for on the wall behind him was a photo from a recent newspaper article. It showed him after his election, at the age of seventy-three, as a Deputy in the Russian Supreme Soviet.

"I stood on a platform of democracy," he proudly told me. "Russia has been an autocracy for centuries, now we are seeing a real revolution. The plague of our society is that it has just stagnated. We have to re-build our entire culture in the broadest sense of the word; from our political culture to our economic, scientific and artistic culture. We need a culture of enlightenment. And at the centre of it all must be a human being . . . this must be the crowning thing."

It was late afternoon when I left, and as I walked along the canal I felt a great sense of hope. What he told me reverberated in my head for weeks afterwards. For all the problems the Soviet Union faces, finally people like this can play a role in the destiny of their country.

The night trains to Moscow left Leningrad every hour, sparks flying off the overhead wires as they shunted out of the station. The Soviet rail system carries four and a half billion passengers a year, and this is its busiest route. It seemed half of Leningrad was travelling to Moscow. Groups of soldiers swaggered by, cigarettes hanging from their mouths. Old couples breathlessly shuffled to their trains dragging huge bags, and lovers attempted passionate goodbyes in the swirling path of the crowd. Once on board it struck me that the curious rituals of train travel are second nature to these people. While I

Russian cities would not be the same without pirozhki sellers and their traditional fried dumplings, with meat, cabbage or potato inside.

fumbled about taking my clothes off for bed, the three Russians I shared my compartment with had all worn sensible tracksuits and were bunked down before we'd even left the station.

The outskirts of Moscow appeared at about eight o'clock the next morning and before long we were passing through a broad, seemingly endless canyon of identical apartment blocks which have multiplied in every Soviet city from Vilnius to Vladivostok like oversized warts. Ten, fifteen stories high, their shoddy and blunt concrete facades make them look as though they've never been finished. At times it appeared that nothing of beauty had been built in this country since the revolution. Even the brutish edifices of the Stalin era took on a certain charm compared to the tacky, pre-fabricated conformity of the "compartment" blocks which vast numbers of Soviet citizens have been herded into. The fields of gargantuan tombstones seem to be a memorial to the death of architecture, and the supremacy of building. I saw their necessity; but quantity, bulk, speed and cheapness have supplanted any notion of aesthetics — not that the West is immune to such problems.

It wasn't a good introduction to Moscow, nor was the dull, grey day which oozed through the city like a stodgy borsch. After being met at the station by a gruff Intourist guide who had trouble tweaking her lips into the faintest of smiles, I began to think that all the clichés about the colourless empire were true.

The Andriuschenko family had been on the night train from Leningrad and lived in an apartment building identical to those we had passed on the way in to Moscow. Ludmilla and Vitaly were both doctors, and their eight-year-old daughter Olga studied music. They had been on a short holiday in Leningrad.

At Moscow Station, one of five major railway stations in Leningrad, trains are notoriously late, as they are throughout the Soviet Union. Sometimes a train will be delayed for hours, but no-one will complain. To do so is a pointless exercise, because those in charge simply blame it on the system. Russians have come to accept inefficiency as a part of daily life.

Despite glasnost, a monolithic bureaucracy still has a hand in every facet of Soviet life, right down to where, and how, people live. The Andriuschenkos had been allocated a three-room flat. It was clean, but like many homes, seemed in a permanent state of semi-darkness. Rent was cheap at twenty roubles a month, but the family needed a bigger flat which they might only get after years of waiting, if they got it at all. The housing shortage is so critical in the Soviet Union, with delays so long, that many families are forced to stay together all their lives. The country's high divorce rate is often blamed on the fact that many newly-weds have no choice but to live with their parents. For the Andriuschenkos it was not so bad, but with Ludmilla's mother living with them, Ludmilla and Vitaly slept in the same room as Olga.

After six years of study, the Andriuschenkos earn less as doctors than the average bus driver. Vitaly is one of Moscow's most skilled neuropathologists, specialising in brain trauma suffered by children. He loves his work and is highly respected, but his wage is only 200 roubles a month. Bus or train drivers earn about 500 roubles. But money isn't the main problem. With cheap housing and nothing to buy, many Russians are rouble rich but commodity poor.

"The most difficult problem is to buy food," said Ludmilla, sitting in the kitchen pouring a cup of black tea. "It's hard to get the food you'd like, and on average, an hour and a half is spent buying food every day. But it's not only the queueing. Time is spent on travelling because you can't buy everything close to home."

Vitaly scratched his goatee in thought. "The most terrible thing for Russians in the past was our fear for the future of our children," he said. "When people said, 'Why do we have such a small number of children?' we answered, 'There's no procreation in prison.' We were very worried about the future of our children. And so, more than anything else, what is happening now gives us hope that with God's help they will be better off. The point is that in this country we were born slaves. We had no way out . . . so I believe glasnost is the most important thing to have occurred during these five years of *perestroika*. Glasnost is a very significant and big achievement. It uplifts people."

Victor Shinkaretsky is middle-aged but one of the new children of glasnost, who uses the recent freedom to criticise to the hilt. A television reporter on a prime time television show, "Good Evening, Moscow!", he has become famous for his scathing exposés of inefficiency, corruption and unsafe work practices. His nickname is "Tomato Joe" after a series of stories he did on contaminated vegetable supplies. The Soviet Union is fertile ground for the investigative journalist. Soft-spoken and unassuming in private, Shinkaretsky is a tenacious bulldog on air. Like Nikita Tolstoy he is fired by an infectious enthusiasm to better his country. And also like Nikita, he was recently voted with a huge majority as a Deputy in the Russian Supreme Soviet.

His story for the night was on milk. In Moscow, supplies are irregular, and when they do come, the milk is thin and watery. With a television crew of two he had walked in unannounced to a Moscow dairy factory to inspect their production methods. His presence created a stir. Workers denied that they were watering down the milk, but confessed that when supplies were low some factories were forced to add water to maintain their production quotas.

"We shouldn't have to put up with these things," he said with genuine anger, raising his voice slightly. "And our society should recognise that it is we who are to blame. No-one wants to fix

For Vitaly and Ludmilla Andriuschenko, both doctors, food shortages and queues are as much a problem as they are for anyone else. But for them, life has become an exercise in spiritual survival. In the pre-glasnost times this kitchen was the only gathering place for their circle of friends where they could discuss anything quietly, but freely.

103

A television reporter and now a Deputy in the Russian parliament, Victor Shinkaretsky ("Tomato Joe") was one of the first media watchdogs unleashed by glasnost — a Soviet Ralph Nader. In Moscow, milk is thin and often bottled in unsanitary conditions. At this dairy factory Shinkaretsky asks an employee why the floors are flooded and unclean. Some eight million people will watch the report on "Good Evening, Moscow!"

anything themselves any more."

Shinkaretsky sees the troubles of the Soviet Union as more profound than simple economics. There are deep-seated problems of psychology. "We are reaping the fruits of Stalin's socialism, of Stalin's conception of socialism, which perverted Lenin's dream," he said. "But the most terrible consequence of Stalin's system wasn't the destruction of the economy, but the destruction of human souls. The morale was destroyed ... the people's spiritual world was destroyed. And now that the policy of perestroika is going ahead it would seem that all we have to do is live, enjoy life. As for work, it turns out that there's no-one to do the work. We've forgotten how to work. All we want is to receive. This is a revolution and no-one will make your revolution for you."

Perhaps it's not surprising that the rate of alcoholism in the Soviet Union is thought to be amongst the highest in the world, with the greatest per capita consumption of distilled spirits. Moscow, like every large Soviet city, has a string of dry-out cells where the police take the inebriated from bars, parks, even their workplaces. The most violent are tied up on beds in dormitories that stink of urine and resound with curses and unruly abuse. When everything else is out of stock, there is always vodka in the shops. It's the one sector of the consumer industry that has generally worked well in the planned economy, but the losses from absenteeism and poor productivity are enormous. After Gorbachev tried to crack down on alcohol consumption in 1985, there was a national sugar shortage, thought to be the result of a huge boom in the production of *samogon*, Russian home-brew. Official estimates put the production of samogon at over a billion litres a year, something of a tribute to the Russian ability to get around the system. It's a measure of desperation, however, that in 1987, ten thousand people died

Above: *With its buskers, painters and political comment, Izmailovsky Park in Moscow is a small test of glasnost. This piece of irreverence is a montage making wicked fun of Soviet slogans and quotable quotes from the speeches of former leaders. "Economy must be economical" (Brezhnev), "Catch up and overtake!" (Krushchev's plan for the USSR), "Life's become better, life's become more fun" (Stalin). Many believe that Gorbachev's much quoted motto "glasnost and perestroika" is just an attempt to boost the morale of a country in deep economic crisis. In fact, the new openness has only served to inform people how bad things really are.*

Left: *Boris Yeltsin, leader of the democratic opposition, poses one of the biggest political threats to Gorbachev. Enormously popular after rejecting many of the comfortable perks that come with power, Yeltsin is nevertheless criticised for being short on policy.*

Above: *A hypnosis session at a Moscow
"Narcological Clinic". Although called a
narcological clinic, drug addicts apart from
alcoholics are a rarity here. While the drug
problem may break out on a large scale in a
not so distant future, it is the alcohol abuse
that claims tens of thousands of lives every
year. Clinics such as this one reveal the scale
of the problem. Apart from hypnosis and
relaxation the clinic offers group and individual
counselling and psychiatric help. Research and
experimentation are conducted, although
treatment rather than mistreatment of addicts
is a relatively new practice.* **Right:** *In Moscow,
landmark buildings represent landmark epochs.
The eccentric onion domes of St Basil's
Cathedral, and the Kremlin behind it, mark
the rule of Ivan the Terrible. In the distance
the 1950s office tower with its gothic flavour,
marks the rule of another tyrant: Joseph Stalin.*

from drinking alcohol substitutes such as perfume, shoe polish and fuels.

The first step on the cobblestones of Red Square sets a film running in your mind which adds a curious double-exposure to everything you see. Anyone who owns a television and watches the news has a mental image, however sketchy, of Red Square and the Kremlin. To actually go there is to bring back a kaleidoscopic flood of images which sign-post the country's history: columns of tanks, goose-stepping soldiers, geriatric leaders and their half-hearted salutes. The curious revelation for the pilgrim to Red Square is that it's much smaller than the mental image. Barely a third the size of Tienanmen Square in Beijing, it hardly seems big enough for the huge military parades that have thundered through here. It's difficult to fathom how Mathias Rust landed his plane on the square in 1987, let alone how he managed to evade the Soviet radar defences.

I was drawn to the unmistakeable focus of Red Square, the thing the Soviet Union chose to place at the spiritual and political heart of the empire. It is the mausoleum which houses the body of Lenin, and despite the calamitous history of the system he introduced, thousands still queue every day for the fleeting opportunity of seeing his sad, waxen body. He is history's most stared at human being. While his image is torn down across Eastern Europe, even in Soviet Georgia, his body remains firmly anchored here.

In a nation of queues, the one before me must have been the longest. It stretched four deep, down along the Kremlin wall, out of Red Square, and out of sight past Alexandrovsky Garden. A good number were tourists, many of the younger ones giggling as if they were queueing for just another attraction at a fun fair, but the majority were Russians, whose mood seemed no more sombre

After Stalin's "reconstruction" of Moscow in 1934, much of the old city was destroyed. In the foreground is the Kremlin wall (it was made of wood until the fifteenth century) and behind it the Bell Tower of Ivan the Great and the Arkhangelsky Cathedral, a few of the buildings that were spared. A Stalin high-rise looms in the distance, a ubiquitous feature in many Soviet cities. The photo was taken from the top of the hotel Rossiya, which itself rose on a site of bulldozed church buildings.

than had they been waiting in line for a pair of shoes. How many come out of mechanical duty, how many come from genuine respect and how many come from the simple curiosity of seeing a dead man in an odd building, is difficult to tell.

Before the taxidermists got to work on Lenin in 1924, there was no precedent in Russian history for embalming the bodies of the country's leaders. In fact the only comparison it bore was with the Russian Orthodox practice of preserving the "relics" of saints. This was a religious gesture of a new kind, the canonisation of the first saint in a new church. There had been an intellectual tendency, particularly strong amongst some Bolsheviks in the giddy days before the revolution, which advocated "God-building". They believed that the proletariat, in creating a more humane society, would cease to be deluded by thoughts of a transcendental God and instead build a "socialist religion of humanity, the most religious of all religions". Despite Lenin's scathing denunciation of such thought, and the desire of both he and his wife that he not be embalmed, the "God-builders" appear to have won. Now there is a growing movement to have Lenin removed from the mausoleum and the Lenin myth deconstructed. Someone's been reading Marx. "The cult of great men is a bourgeoisie myth," he wrote.

As the queue drew closer to the monolithic solemnity of the marble tomb, chatter fell away and people straightened up. Hands were pulled from pockets and dangled awkwardly trying to find the right expression for the occasion; respectfully held behind or reverentially clasped at the front? Finally, everyone fell silent. I felt as if I'd walked into a Catholic church and stumbled into communion. But once past the bronze doors, with the relentless flow of the crowd pushing me down the gloomy

passage-way, it was more like boarding a ghost train where no-one was allowed to scream. My eyes struggled to adjust to the dimness, then without warning, his head and hands suddenly appeared in a pool of unnaturally white light. Lenin's face was pale, with a dull sheen of waxiness on its Tatar cheekbones that didn't seem remotely human. The hair was thinner and lighter than I'd imagined. This corpse was a far cry from the swashbuckling Lenin depicted on countless billboards and statues across the country. I'd seen stuffed animals more life-like. It was just a head and hands, as unreal as the formal stiffness of the body they were attached to. I began to wonder what this man would now think of the country he helped create, but there was no stopping to allow speculation of any kind. To do so would only invite unhealthy thoughts about the absurdity and indignity of such a ritual. Human beings weren't meant for this.

A moment later I was shunted out of Lenin's mausoleum into the daylight and found myself walking by the graves along the Kremlin wall, to be confronted immediately by the bust of Stalin. Before history caught up with his deeds, Stalin shared the mausoleum with Lenin between 1953 and 1961, a fact that would likely have abhorred Lenin, who described Stalin as "too rude", a defect "intolerable in a General Secretary". Some would say that Stalin's grave is still too grand. All that Nikita Tolstoy had told me about the Stalin years, all that I had read, came flooding back as I stood before the proud arrogance of his bust. I walked away in disgust.

I crossed the square to GUM, the state-owned shopping emporium which faces the Kremlin. It's a grand, three-tiered series of arcades painted in blue and pink with wrought-iron walkways spanning each section. A delightful, suffused light, spills from long arched skylights. It's a temple to consumerism,

At Lenin's Mausoleum the guard of honour (Number 1 Post) has gone through this same ritual since the leader of the revolution died in 1924. His embalmed body was first placed in a wooden mausoleum, before the granite one he now resides in was completed in 1930. A deified figure for decades, there is a growing movement to have Lenin removed from the mausoleum and buried in a normal grave as was his wish. If that happens it may well signal the final defeat of a moribund ideology.

with little to sell. Shelves looked sad and empty. Shoppers only seemed to muster enthusiasm for things foreign. I spent fifteen minutes struggling through the queues and crowds, looking for somewhere to eat, but there was no sign of a cafe or restaurant. Undeterred, I made my way towards Gorky Street, which sweeps up off Red Square away from the Moscow River. But to cross from Red Square to the main footpath was an impossible task, for there before me was a dauntingly wide road carrying a sea of traffic in which the pedestrian did not figure. Moscow seemed full of these race-ways, broad stretches of unlined bitumen, which often demanded walking hundreds of metres out of your way to find an underground crossing. In some parts cars have few qualms about mounting the curb and using the pedestrian walkway as an extra lane of traffic. Only in Los Angeles did the tyranny of the car seem greater.

When finally I reached Gorky Street, it was little more welcoming. Whereas the commerce and colour of Western cities bubbles over, here there seemed to be a strange vacuum. And this in one of Moscow's busiest streets. Shops were sparse and identified only by blunt, utilitarian signs which said "meat" or "dairy". Snaking from them were the ubiquitous queues of morose looking Russians. They were part of a strangely private crowd which had no time for frivolity or laughter. I remembered Ludmilla's comment that the enduring struggle for most people was just finding food, in fact, thirty per cent of the population lives below the official poverty line. The indignity of it all depressed me. It was as if a few scraps had been thrown on the ground, and like chickens in a coop, the Russians would frantically race from one pile to the next to scrounge what they could.

After some time looking, I eventually passed a half-empty restaurant and quickly made my way to the front door. Through the glass I caught sight of the doorman, a short man whose bulldog chest filled out every fold of his dark suit. He swung the door open, but before I even had a chance to ask for a table the world "nyet" spat from his mean mouth. No smile, no explanation, no apology, just "nyet". The door slammed shut in my face. I wasn't sure whether to laugh or take offence, but after a few more minutes trudging through the cold wind on Gorky Street the same thing happened. The pattern had been familiar through much of Eastern Europe. Indeed, there was a blunt logic in discouraging patrons. Every customer meant extra work, but extra work didn't mean extra money. The wage came if the restaurant was empty or full. But here, in the main street of the capital, at the very apex of Soviet civilisation, I had expected things to be better. What hope is there for any economy, which despite *perestroika,* still has trouble delivering the simple efficiency required to run restaurants?

I never thought I'd be glad to see a McDonald's sign, but there, off in the distance near Pushkin Square, it beckoned. At the point of desperation, salivating already at the thought of a sickly sweet burger between my teeth, I strode up the street with a renewed sense of purpose. Only then did I discover that the longest queue in Moscow, after the queue for Lenin's mausoleum, was at McDonald's. It is always full, from the moment it opens, to the second it shuts. It must rank as the busiest hamburger shop in the world. I walked away in despair and bought a cold salami at a nearby shop.

A short distance from Gorky Street, I caught a train to one of the extraordinary underground palaces that make up Moscow's metro system, emerging at Dzerzhinsky Square. Felix Dzerzhinsky claims the dubious honour of being

Left above: *Queueing is a way of life all over the Soviet Union. Ironically, an absence of a queue is not a good sign. Where there are queues there is something to be bought. No queue, no food. In a country where you go shopping for what you can get, not what you want, it's no wonder people often join queues without knowing what's for sale.*
Left below: *When shops aren't literally empty, they are often stocked with things nobody wants. In this fish shop there is no fresh fish; just cans of sprats, spiced sprats and "mintai", all highly unpopular fish which never attract a queue.*

A scene from Christmas-time in Red Square. Members of the "Telephone Pioneers of America" visit and sing Christmas carols. Although the Soviet government abolished Christmas from the calendar because it was a religious festival, many people simply celebrated the occasion on New Year's Eve instead. Father Christmas' attire was inherited by the perfectly secular "Grandpa Frost" who arrived from Russian folklore to replace his predecessor. The Grandpa, dressed in red, visits children on New Year's Eve and leaves them surprises under a decorated fir-tree. This scene took place directly in front of the Lenin Mausoleum (with the Kremlin wall in the background).

*11 December 1989: the Day of Human Rights.
At a rally for democracy in Moscow a protester
holds a placard with the words "ATTENTION!
DEMOCRACY HAS BEEN VIOLATED".
Real freedom of thought and speech is taking
over the artificial notion of glasnost (officially
condoned or even encouraged, public discussion).
But as Soviet citizens are often at pains to
point out to the West, so long as there is no
legislation making the new developments
irreversible, they are not safe.*

Right: *Gypsy children join in a dance with an
elderly woman in the easy-going atmosphere of
Arbat Street, a pedestrian mall where artists,
onlookers and the so-called "informals" like to
spend their moments of leisure. Arbat was a
favourite Moscow district for many writers and
poets. Its main street has recently been
renovated, to attract tourists and hard currency.*

founder of the KGB — the successor to
Lenin's own secret police, the CHEKA —
and his statue commands centre stage in
a busy roundabout of traffic. Behind it is
an innocuous looking building just ten
stories high, but with an unknown
number of floors below. It is the
headquarters of the KGB. I had made a
point of visiting the existing, or former,
temples of repression in Eastern Europe
and this was the father of them all. The
role of the KGB has become less sinister
under Gorbachev, indeed many say it has
ceased to be an instrument of political
repression and has turned to nuts and
bolts crime fighting. But while that may
be true, its presence still weighs heavily
in the minds of the Soviet people.
Hidden in the bowels of the building is
Lubyanka Prison, the most notorious in
the Soviet Union. Entering Lubyanka
through the black gates at the rear of the
building was the first stop on the way to
Siberia for many people. For others, it
meant a bullet in the back of the head. It
had heard the whispers of people
denouncing friends, the forced
confessions of uncommitted crimes. I
imagined the building as a giant factory
of human misery, one which had few
equals in history.

Returning through the grey drizzle to
my hotel, I found myself getting more
and more depressed. The brutish
doorman with a brace of Second World
War medals on his chest, who accusingly
demanded my hotel registration slip each
time I walked in, only made things
worse. When I went to the hotel
restaurant for dinner the waitress
shrugged her shoulders when I asked for
a table and walked away. I retreated to my
room, and looking through the grotty
panes of double glass at the procession
of trucks carrying pre-fabricated
concrete blocks for yet another
anonymous apartment block, I fell into a
well of misery.

I didn't want to be negative about the

Rock fans at an International Peace Festival in Moscow's Lenin Stadium. With overseas bands like Bon Jovi and Motley Crew and top acts from the Soviet Union, this concert still stands as one of the biggest in the country's history. These people were lucky enough to get a ticket, while many fans listen from outside the stadium. Rock music has surged ahead in the Soviet Union, with bands like Brigada S and Gorky Park, becoming immensely popular. While their music is derivative of rock in the West, none have yet cracked the international market.

Soviet Union, but I had found so little joy here, and so many problems, that it was hard to feel otherwise. It seemed impossible to penetrate the gruff exterior of the place; everything appeared twisted and upside down. The most simple of day-to-day dealings, the countless encounters and transactions that keep life rolling along, were poisoned by the rudeness of an unhappy people. But it was for them that I felt most sorrow. They had lived through a social experiment which had become a fraud to its own ideals. It had failed in even the most basic task of adequately feeding and housing its citizens. There were many satellites, but little soap. To think of the country's history, and the daily humiliations people still lived with, I couldn't help but see it all as a massive assault on human dignity.

I tried to call home, and after two hours of constant dialling, managed to get through to the international operator. I asked to make a call to Australia. "I'm sorry, sir," the operator replied. "This is not possible. Could you call back the day after tomorrow?"

All I could do was laugh.

My last morning in Moscow pleasantly changed my impressions of the city, for it was then that I discovered a Moscow I had missed the day before. In a few short hours on Arbat Street and in Izmailovsky Park, there was a life and vitality I hadn't seen earlier. Here I found splashes of colour and ripples of laughter. Side by side with a burgeoning number of street traders, buskers and comics satirised the country's dilemmas.

One comic wheeled out a joke I'd heard as far away as East Germany: "'What is the basis of the Soviet economic system?', the political instructor asked the worker. 'You pretend to pay us, and we pretend to work'." Crowds laughed at the sight of a man wearing a mask of Leonard Brezhnev, the leader the Soviet people universally despise for the dull era of stagnation he presided over. Stalin, Kruschev, Gorbachev, all were mercilessly lampooned. Indeed, the only Soviet leader absent from this tirade was Lenin. Such public displays of political criticism were unheard of until the past few years, but in that simple freedom to criticise lay the means to a new future.

There had been some publicity for a large rock concert at Lenin Stadium, site of the 1980 Moscow Olympics, and before my train left I decided to walk past and take in some of the atmosphere. Any rock concert is an unusual event in the Soviet Union, but this one was billed as "a heavy metal meltdown for world peace" with top local bands and headline acts from the United States. From outside, the catchy melody of a Russian pop song had my foot tapping, and when it ended there was a mountainous roar of clapping and screaming from the crowd. It was an antidote to yesterday's gloom . . . a gloriously loud expression of simple joy.

The Rossiya, *pride of the Soviet rail system. Each day*
Rossiya *Number 1 arrives at the Yaroslavl Station,*
having travelled almost 10,000 kilometres from
Vladivostok, on the Pacific coast in the Far East. And
each day Rossiya *Number 2 departs in the opposite*
direction. It is a seven-day journey, and at any one time
there are fourteen Rossiyas *plying back and forth across*
the country.

CHAPTER FOUR

EXILE AND THE NEW TEXAS

Moscow to Novosibirsk

Yaroslavl Station looks less like a railway station and more like a giant gingerbread house. It's a surprising splash of eccentricity in Moscow's dourness, but a fitting one. As the hub of the largest rail network on earth, Yaroslavl Station is a shunting yard for a cast of fairytale characters reflecting the fifteen republics and hundreds of ethnic groups that make up the Soviet empire. From the Turkish looks of the Armenians, to the white skin and sharp features of the Byelorussians (White Russians), there's a swirling mass of Europeans, Asians and everyone in between. Stand here long enough and the entire Soviet Union comes and goes.

This is the starting point of the Trans-Siberian Express, a journey so loaded with the mental baggage of myth, legend and romance, that you cart it around like a second suitcase. It has gained this unique status because it is a journey of extremes: extremely long, extremely cold, extremely frustrating, extremely interesting and extremely boring. The Mohammed Ali of train travel, it holds the undisputed title of longest train journey in the world, plodding through seven time zones and nearly a hundred degrees of longitude. Even New York to Los Angeles, via New Orleans on the Sunset Limited is less than half the distance. Vladivostok, the Soviet warm-water port on the Sea of Japan, is almost 10,000 kilometres away and to travel its length takes seven full days. But the most exotic musings are triggered by one word: Siberia.

This intoxicating melange of fact and mystery bubbled away at the back of my

Tradition and necessities of life send hordes of people to Moscow for shopping when the regional shops are understocked. Something that may be termed "the bag phenomenon" is inescapable at railway stations, such as here, outside Yaroslavl Railway Station in Moscow. Moscow was always better provided for than the rest of the country, and it still has that reputation despite severe food shortages and even rationing.

mind as I walked into the cavernous belly of Yaroslavl Station. There was almost no natural light, with huge chandeliers struggling to illuminate the smoke-filled dimness. As I went in further, I thought I'd stumbled not into a railway station, but a refugee camp. For it appeared people weren't actually waiting but living here. Rather than arriving an hour or so before their train departed, it seemed they had come days earlier, or were caught in transit limbo between ill-matched connections. Whole families had barricaded themselves into their own private space by a wall of baggage, and sat sawing away at oily salamis and huge black loaves of bread, as if they had just begun the evening meal at home. Babies hung off mothers' breasts. Snoring bodies lay sprawled on wooden benches, some on the floor, totally oblivious to the cacophony of hacking coughs, screaming children and the hubbub of hundreds of conversations. These people seemed to be the bread and butter of the Soviet Union, the proletariat in whose name the revolution had been called.

I side-stepped my way through the crowd and onto the platform. Off into the distance stretched the twenty green carriages of the Trans-Siberian Express with a brutish VL80 (Vladimir Lenin) class electric engine mounted at the front. With coal *samovars* smoking from each carriage, the train seemed alive, expiring whooshes of compressed air like a horse eager to bolt. Each carriage was embellished with a metal plaque bearing a gold hammer and sickle against a yellow globe. Golden sheaves of wheat carried the names of the Soviet Republics and, above all this, a red star. But beneath each plaque was a small sign which was far more evocative. As the pride of the Russian rail system the train bore the name of the country: *Rossiya*. And beneath it, in Cyrillic, the magic words: MOSCOW – VLADIVOSTOK.

The door to each carriage was flanked by a welcoming committee (or unwelcoming committee depending on your luck) of two *provodniks*, the attendants who take turns working the twelve-hour shifts for the entire journey. I gave my ticket to a ferocious-looking young woman, then lumbered aboard the train. The first thing that struck me as I slid open the door to my four-berth, second class, compartment was the overwhelming, sweet and sour smell of dirty socks. I had expected body odours on this trip — there are no showers on the Trans-Siberian — but not quite so soon. Within seconds, my notion of the journey as romantic was being quickly recategorised into the earthier realm of adventure. The socks belonged to two Russian men who looked a little dismayed at the arrival of a problematic foreigner as their travelling companion. Both had stripped down to tracksuit pants and singlets, and were sprawled out on their double-bunk as if they had been on the train for days.

As the provodniks flagged the all-clear, the train's couplings clunked together and we gently swayed from side to side out of Moscow as if sitting astride a lumbering elephant. It was drizzling, and grey, and the apartment blocks and factories looked bleaker than usual through the dirty glass. I looked across at the older Russian sitting opposite and his round Tatar face. He looked friendly enough, but when I noticed a set of numbers roughly tattooed across the back of his hand and a deformed nail on his forefinger which twisted around like an eagle's talon, I felt a little uneasy. He reached into his pocket and produced a knife. Suddenly I had visions of my throat being sliced open and my body being found beside the tracks in the depths of Siberia. He pulled some bread and sausage from his bag. I relaxed.

"Pa Russki?" he asked, looking up.
'Nyet,' I replied, shrugging my

An integral part of the Soviet railway system, provodniks are more than just conductors, especially on the Trans-Siberian. From the moment they take your ticket to the moment you step off the train, they can make your journey a misery or a joy. Provodniks provide tea, bedding and keep the train clean. Get off-side with your provodnik and the longest train journey in the world can become a nightmare.

shoulders. "Pa Anglee'skee?" "Nyet," he smiled, then called up to his friend. "Boris, pa Anglee'skee?" Boris swung around on his bunk. "Hello very much. I Boris. I Misha."

After a few minutes of incomprehensible blundering we realised there were probably no more than ten words between us we both understood. I cursed myself for not having a phrasebook with anything more useful than: "Which way to the museum please?" or "What do I do about my luggage?" It was going to be a long trip. But with the simplest of introductions complete, we were suddenly comrades and I was flattered by the invitation to share their meal. It was robust fare. The sausage seemed no better than that described by Chekhov during a journey across Siberia in 1890: "When you put a piece in your mouth it's filled with a stench as though you had entered a stable at the very moment when the drivers are removing their foot cloths." The fishpaste was worse, making the compartment smell less like a dirty laundry and more like the bowels of a fishing trawler. Then, with a mischievous grin, Misha leant across, locked the door and pulled a bottle of vodka from the bottom of his bag. Alcohol is forbidden on Soviet trains, so with the shared naughtiness of school kids smoking behind the toilet doors, we took turns swigging from the bottle. Russians are masters at beating the system and delight in doing so. As the vodka worked its giddy magic, Boris switched on the radio, unleashing the relentless beat of a Russian pop song which I was to come to know painfully well. With the outskirts of Moscow fast receding, the three of us slipped into a pleasant reverie where language was irrelevant, but a simple camaraderie established.

Seventy kilometres from Moscow, the train rattled into the outskirts of a small, rustic town and then burst unexpectedly

Left: *The world's longest railway journey soon becomes just that. Time becomes a meaningless blur. Seven days sharing the same compartment can forge or break friendships. An escape into the corridor can only be temporary.* **Above:** *The rural landscape flashes past the window of the* **Rossiya.**

onto a glorious forest of spires, surrounded by blue and gilded domes. Gleaming against the grey sky, they were topped with glittering gold crosses and studded with gold stars. This was Zagorsk, religious capital of Russia and home of the Trinity Monastery of St Sergius. With its seminary and academy for young priests, the monastery is the headquarters of the Russian Orthodox Church. The monastery was rebuilt after being burnt down by the Tatars in 1408, but more miraculously, later survived the assault of communism. In 1919 the stated programme of the Communist Party was clear: "To liberate the toiling masses from religious prejudices and to organise the broadest scientific – educational and anti-religious propaganda." But the "liberation" took the form of simple destruction. Thousands of churches across the Soviet Union were demolished after the revolution, bibles and icons were burnt in a fervour as fanatic as any religious zealot's. Priests were arrested with a large number simply executed by the CHEKA (secret police) as class enemies. A similar fate befell Muslims, Catholics, Jews, Buddhists and Baptists. Any religion was an intolerable rival to the new religion of communism. The Trinity Monastery of St Sergius remained intact partly because it was declared a museum in 1920. Despite the indignity of having the capital of the Orthodox Church renamed Zagorsk, after a communist revolutionary with a Jewish background, this may have further helped secure the monastery's survival.

Apart from a brief respite during the war years, it has only been in the past five years that religious persecution has lifted in the Soviet Union. Right across the country you come across churches being restored, slowly rescued from the ignominy of their conversion to shops or museums.

I had seen a little of the passion some Russians feel for their religion when I visited Novodevichy Convent in Moscow. It was a regular weekday service, but crowded to overflowing with a congregation made up almost exclusively of old women cowled with scarves. Stunted with age, they slowly shuffled about the church crossing themselves and murmuring prayers with intense concentration. One old woman in black, with a crutch under one arm and a walking stick in her other hand, spent half an hour kissing the foot of a small statue of Christ. Even for the non-believer, the service was uplifting. Sung by a small choir, the liturgy had as sweet a refrain as I'd ever heard and behind the iconostasis, through a large doorway, bearded priests drifted back and forth like wizards in a mystical theatre of robes, candles and incense.

My four-berth shoebox on the Trans-Siberian was also removed from the world outside, and while hardly heavenly, it was pleasant enough. After frantic attempts to pull down the window and dilute the smell of socks and fishpaste, I discovered it was screwed shut against the cold, like all windows on the train. No amount of pleading with the provodnik could open it, and only a stuntman would consider finding fresh air by standing in the draughty walkway between carriages. The prospect of a seven day journey without showers was one thing, seven days without fresh air didn't bear thinking about.

Half a day out of Moscow, as we drifted by flat, gentle country of flax and potato farming, there was still novelty in the rituals and routines of train travel, and amongst the most welcome were the glasses of black Russian tea brought by a provodnik, always with a few cubes of sugar, and sometimes a small packet of armour-plated biscuits if you were lucky. The water for the tea came from the coal-fired samovars at the front of each carriage, bizarre contraptions with a tangle of pipes and gauges. The service

"The Birth of Christ", a fragment of the vault painting in the Zagorsk Uspensky church (built 1559–1585). Thirty-five painters worked on the church murals in 1684.

Left: *A priest conducting a service in the Uspensky church in Zagorsk, headquarters of the Russian Orthodox Church. Recently the government has relaxed its oppressive attitudes and is making an effort to be cooperative with the Russian Orthodox patriarchy. Religious revival is strongly felt. Churches are being opened up and renovated, though this tends to affect mostly the churches in the public eye. Above: Believers reaching out for the cross during a Transfiguration service in a Russian Orthodox Church in Zagorsk.*

never seemed to conform to any discernible routine. Getting a cup of tea appeared to rely more on the mood of the provodnik than anything else. Maintaining good relations with one's provodnik takes on special importance.

As for Boris and Misha, hours of pained conversation with frequent resort to charades and stick drawing had revealed what would normally take five minutes had we spoken the same language. Misha was in his mid-thirties, a basketball coach, married with a son. He shared the common feeling among many Russians that Gorbachev talked too much and hadn't delivered on *perestroika*. Boris was twenty-two, worked in a factory and liked pop music. Both were returning to Novosibirsk after a shopping trip to Moscow. It was a journey of two days and two nights each way, and the boxes of ghetto-blasters stashed away above their beds indicated they probably dabbled in a little private trading. As dinner approached I rose to make my way to the dining-car, but at the insistence of Boris and Misha joined them for another dose of fishpaste, making a small contribution by way of English tea-bags which they had never seen before, and which Misha duly pocketed for display to his wife.

That night, in the overbearing stuffiness of the compartment with Boris snoring above me, I roused myself as the *Rossiya* clanked across a long bridge. Peering into the darkness, I caught a few flashes of light reflecting off the water and realised we were crossing that great Russian landmark, the Volga. In times past, Russian men would stand and doff their hats when they crossed. It was a salute to Mother Volga, a river steeped in folklore, and as important to Russia as the Nile is to Egypt.

The Volga is the longest river in Europe and has long been a source of food and a major thoroughfare for shipping. It rises in the Valday Hills,

Above: *The* **Rossiya** *is a very long train ...*
Above right: *The once great "Mother Volga" has known better times. Many old villages were buried under water when a dam was created here, and industries have caused a bad pollution problem. People still sing songs about the Volga River and of the heroes that crossed it to conquer lands.* **Below right:** *The city square of Kazan, capital of the Tatar Autonomous Republic. Kazan was once a great capital in the period of the Golden Hordes, founded in the thirteenth century on the Volga and Kazanka Rivers. When Ivan the Terrible defeated the Hordes in 1552 Kazan was annexed to Russia.*

A Kazan street scene which probably looked little different fifty years ago. The Soviet Union has a First World army, but the rest of society remains caught in a time-warp.

north of Moscow, and flows 3700 kilometres into the Caspian Sea, where it fans into five hundred branches at its vast delta. Every drop flows through Soviet territory. But today, choked with agricultural and industrial pollution, the pride of the country is in a sad state. In the lower reaches of the Volga, sturgeon are now found floating belly-up in shoals before they can spawn their precious caviar.

Also on the banks of the Volga, is Kazan, capital of the Tatar Autonomous Republic. Founded in 1399, Kazan was the great stronghold of the Golden Hordes who terrorised Russia before Ivan the Terrible set about unifying the country and conquered them in 1552. The Tatars were semi-nomadic cattlemen from Central Asia, made up of Turks and the dreaded Mongols. While some still believe they are a violent people, for four centuries now they have lived side by side with the Russians without any major tension although there is rising nationalism. Amongst the faces of Kazan's one million people it's sometimes easy to pick the Tatars. The Imam's evening call to prayer is evidence their Islamic faith still survives in the region today, despite the systematic repression Moslems were subjected to after the revolution of 1917.

But Kazan now has different tensions, ones well-known to the West. There are estimated to be over three hundred youth gangs in the city and last year, fifteen people died in a plague of youth violence with parallels in urban ghettos around the world. The causes are hard to define, but Nikolai Morosov, a local film-maker who has documented the problem, claims the alienation of modern Soviet housing, frustration with the system and loss of traditions all contribute.

"It begins as a game," he says, "kids fighting over their playground. They start getting involved in petty crime, and

Above: *A stallholder at Kazan "free" market. Prices are high here, and no matter how much you bargain, the sums are unimaginable compared to prices in official stores. Fruit and vegetables can cost ten times more than in government shops, but the range and quality is better. Much of the produce comes from central Asia and is brought in illegally. Corruption is taken for granted and the authorities turn a blind eye. Right: A salesman at the Kazan markets, with the typical features of a Tatar.*

Top Right: *A village on the Trans-Siberian railway not far from Kazan. It has become an institution in the Soviet Union for groups to be sent from a workplace or an institute to help out on state farms. While doing this they are paid their usual wages (students are supposed to do it for fun). These people have been picking potatoes.*

Bottom right: *The Tatars are the sixth largest ethnic group in the Soviet Union. Most Tatars are Muslim, along with at least ten other ethnic groups in the country (in fact, every fifth person in the Soviet Union is Muslim!). Yet until recently there was only one open mosque in Kazan, and both religious and nationalist groups here are fighting for self-determination.*

Left: *Alienation, frustration and loss of tradition all contribute to an increase in problems amongst urban youth across the Soviet Union. These boys are members of one of Kazan's three hundred youth gangs. Violence between the gangs is endemic.*

Above: *"I love my love, because my love loves me." When a war veteran comes up to you in the middle of nowhere and starts reciting Shakespeare in perfect English, you begin to understand many Russians profound love of literature. From Pletnyovka village near Kazan, Mikhail Ivanovich Rodionov learnt English as a technical translator in a military school. He now maintains it by listening to the BBC and "Voice of America".*

before long they are used by organised crime in running protection rackets. Exactly why they are so violent is difficult to explain. A person can live all his life in Kazan and never encounter this problem. But when he begins to run into this trouble, when it reaches out and touches him, and his family, then he begins to comprehend just how frightening it is."

For more than a thousand kilometres east of Moscow the journey is pancake flat, with never a chance to rise above the landscape to gain even a little perspective. But it is rarely boring. Countless villages drift by the windows: lonely, self-contained little settlements with rows of sturdy Russian farmhouses (*izbah*) built of pine logs, their quaint windows with their detailed fretwork painted blue or green. The larger villages may have a wooden church, others are as small as a dozen houses only. Roads are rutted stretches of mud, piles of rubbish lie scattered about, cars, even tractors, are an uncommon sight. If they are representative of the typical Russian village, then the lot of the villager is not easy. And for all the hyperbole of collectivisation and five-year plans, Russian villages still share the malaise rural villages suffer in any developing country. Young people leave to work in the cities. They take their vigour, and leave an air of desertion and decay.

Finally, almost imperceptibly, the Trans-Siberian begins to climb. Two days and 1500 kilometres out of Moscow begin the Urals, Russia's most famous mountain range which divides the entire continent. The mountains almost succeed in stretching from the Arctic Ocean in the north, to the Caspian Sea in the south, but their length is more impressive than their height, for where the rail crosses, they manage to rise to only 994 metres. At their highest points in the north they struggle to almost 2000

metres. Winding through the hills, across deep cuttings, now we could see both ends of the *Rossiya* at the same time. As we gradually climbed higher the forests of aspen and birch slowly gave way to pines, some of them immense trees, with snow still hugging their bases. In each village timber yards lined the track. Freight trains stacked with logs raced in the opposite direction towards Moscow.

Seventeen hundred and seventy-seven kilometres from Moscow there is a fleeting glimpse of a white obelisk on the southern side of the train. It is the dividing line of two worlds. On one side, in Cyrillic, is the word EUROPE, and on the other, ASIA. It also marks the western boundary of Siberia, and as the exiles passed this point they described it as "passing beyond the pillar of tears". It was a melancholy thought to imagine the millions of souls, before the revolution and after, who had passed this same point, never to return. Crammed in foul-smelling prison trains or cattle trucks, separated from their families, they were condemned to end their lives in labour camps. In *The Gulag Archipeligo,* Solzhenitsyn's account of life in Stalin's Gulag or labour camps, he described the trains carrying prisoners as "the ships of the archipeligo". Often the prison carriages (*zak* cars) were attached to the end of a normal passenger train

"The train starts — and a hundred crowded prisoner destinies, tormented hearts, are borne along the same snaky rails, behind the same smoke, past the same fields, posts and haystacks as you . . . And in the familiar life of the train, which is always exactly the same — with its slit-openable package of bed linen, and the tea served in glasses with metal holders — could you possibly grasp what a dark and suppressed horror has been borne through the same sector of Euclidean space . . . "

As the *Rossiya* clatters down the Urals and into the western fringes of

A weary babushka sits outside her house in a Russian village on the Volga, not far from Kazan. The villages are dying out. Young people leave for the cities and there is no-one left to maintain the household. If old people move to the city they find it hard to survive on a pension of about 50 roubles a month.

Siberia, you begin to appreciate the magnitude, not only of the country, but of the railway that straddles it. For as incomprehensibly vast as the forests of birch beside you are the forests of sleepers beneath you. While the British colonised their empire by sea, the Russians colonised theirs by rail. Building a line to Vladivostok opened up the vast resources of Siberia and strengthened control over the Far East. Before the railway, the only route across Siberia was the Trakt, or Great Siberian Post Road, a glorified trail of mud and snow. It took the Czar's couriers sixteen days to travel the 5825 kilometres between Irkutsk and St Petersburg, but using two hundred changes of horses, they were considerably faster than the ordinary traveller. Until the mid-1890s, when large sections of the Trans-Siberian were completed, it was quicker to travel from Vladivostok to St Petersburg by crossing the Pacific Ocean, North America and the Atlantic Ocean, than by travelling west across Siberia.

Built today, the Trans-Siberian would be a remarkable achievement, but built ninety years ago, without the aid of heavy machinery, it ranks as one of the great engineering feats of the century. The first sod was turned in 1891 and by 1895 almost seventy thousand men, from Chinese coolies to convicts, were laying 4 kilometres of track a day. Work was finally completed in 1916, the last year of the Czar's rule, at a total cost of about $US500 million. The whole line has now been electrified, a massive undertaking in itself. Traversing a quarter of the earth's circumference, there is enough track on the railway to stretch a single line of metal right around the world.

Early accounts of travel on the Trans-Siberian describe comforts that have long disappeared. First class sleepers featured a communal lounge with overstuffed armchairs, a small library and even a piano, for which there seemed no

shortage of musicians. There were buzzers in each compartment to summon waiters, an individually regulated heating system and each train had a barber, a small dispensary and live fish in tanks for cooking by the chef. Reading such details brings on a pronounced melancholy in today's traveller. It has since become a more utilitarian enterprise, the East-German built carriages adequately comfortable, but hardly luxurious.

More important is the access the Trans-Siberian has given to the country's most valuable resource: oil. First discovered in Siberia in 1965, the daily output of 12.1 million barrels makes the Soviet Union the world's largest oil producer. It is also the world's second largest exporter, with oil and gas exports accounting for over half of Soviet hard currency earnings. If Siberia is the New Texas, then its Houston is Tyumen. Capital of the Tyumenskaya Oblast, Tyumen administers a region that produces sixty per cent of Soviet oil. It is Siberia's oldest city, founded in 1586, and in the days before the railway was better known as a forwarding post for criminals and exiles who were shipped in crowded prison barges to Tomsk on the River Ob.

Much of the development in Siberia was undertaken during the Brezhnev era when the development of heavy industry gained its enduring ascendancy over the production of simple consumer goods. While the rest of the country stagnated, in Siberia there was a feverish "gigantomania". Brezhnev poured billions of roubles into huge dams, mines and oilfields — the bigger the better — which were often ill-conceived and poorly planned. While the oil industry in Siberia has been a great source of wealth, rampant exploitation and a failing infrastructure have led to one of the Soviet Union's greatest environmental disasters. This in a place most people still imagine as an untouched wilderness.

Every second 12 tons of oil are pumped out of the Tyumen region which provides up to sixty per cent of the USSR's oil and gas. In a chase for higher production figures, the government encouraged more drilling even when it was still possible to extract oil from the existing wells. These "bushes" have sprouted over the Siberian landscape. Accidents are numerous. The spills are either burned out or left to be soaked up by the earth in a hope that the earth will accept back what it has produced. But nothing grows here, and it is not certain if the land will ever recover.

The construction of the Trans-Siberian railway remains one of the great engineering feats of the last hundred years. Begun in 1891 and completed in 1916 (the last year of the Czar's rule), hundreds of thousands of peasants, convicts and new settlers provided the labour. At one point, 4 kilometres of track was being laid each day by seventy thousand men, without the aid of heavy machinery. Transversing a quarter of the earth's circumference, there is enough track on the railway to stretch a single line of metal right around the world.

Building the massive bridges over the

wide Siberian rivers involved the most sophisticated engineering. This bridge over the Yenisey River was one of the longest and most difficult, with six main spans, it stretched almost a kilometre.

The Trans-Siberian Express was said to be the "jewel in the crown of the Czars". Shown here is the Russian empress's sleeping chamber (right) and the salon (left) in the Czar's own train. But even the average train was luxurious, with its electric lights, restaurant, library, lounge car with piano, bathrooms and ladies boudoir. These days there are few frills on the Trans-Siberian.

In the editorial office of *Tyumen Komsomolets*, Tyumen's largest newspaper, environmental issues now feature at each weekly news conference. The paper's circulation has trebled since glasnost, with frank articles on social issues, corruption and the environment. But while such stories have been mainstream news in the West for almost ten years, glasnost has uncovered a litany of environmental problems which carry an even greater urgency because they have been both neglected and suppressed.

"Two years ago no-one was working on ecological issues," says the paper's female environmental reporter, Alla Pozhidayeva. "Even the word 'ecology' was rarely mentioned. We began to intrude into spheres that were earlier closed to us, we were simply not allowed to come close to them. The worst problem in our region is the oil industry; everything's leaking, everything's spilling, everything's being dropped on the ground, in rivers. People live with that tragedy."

Eight hundred kilometres north-east of Tyumen, some of Siberia's largest oil fields surround the city of Nizhnevartovsk. Home to a quarter of a million people enticed by a wage loading to come here and work, it is a flat, bleak place; a lonely field of apartment blocks rising out of the dust. Encircling the town like a herd of prehistoric animals are thousands of pumps, slowly bobbing up and down, drinking oil from the earth. More oil is produced in this region than in Saudi Arabia. Pipelines head straight to Europe and into the cars of the West, but much of the oil never reaches its destination. Outdated and corroded, the pipelines often burst, reportedly sending millions of barrels of oil spilling out into the forests. Thousands of square kilometres of forest have been destroyed by subsequent fires and poisoning of the soil. You can fly for hours above the

Above: *Bore-hole driller Baudi Shoukhaloz from Nizhnevartovsk. Baudi has been living in this region for ten years and has seen Lake Samotlor die and the forest disintegrate. He says: "We say now that what's been done was because of the stagnation period. It's not our fault. But just as we blame the old people for all this stagnation, we'll be blamed for destroying nature." He wishes there was more efficiency and less wanton destruction, but he likes his job because it's a real man's job, he says.* **Left:** *Life out of sync. A street scene in Nizhnevartovsk. These apartment blocks in Nizhnevartovsk are for the lucky oil industry workers. In the oil industry, two hundred thousand workers, most of them with families, are waiting for a home. Many live in wooden shacks.*

Right: *A cemetery of scorched cedar trees spreads for 10,000 hectares. It resulted from a huge forest fire in the summer which started at the site of a small oilspill near an oilwell. It will take decades to regenerate, if ever.*
Far right: *Vladimir, from Bashkiriya, has been working on the oil rigs for six years. He says it has become frightening to work here. A major accident is possible any minute. While fixing a leak in an oil pipe, he said there were more accidents every year as the equipment became more worn out. The standards have fallen. In the past a small break would cause an urgent visit from the authorities. Now numerous accidents are not even reported.*

Petroleum gas burning at the area of the oil-rich Lake Samotlor, in
Tyumen region. Since oil was discovered in this region in the 1960s
an unprecedented boom has ensued. The industry promised the
country untold riches and was built up in an atmosphere of
euphoria, but the money and the promises have gone up in smoke.
Thousands of kilometres of underground piping slowly rotted, but
the problems below the surface were not taken into consideration by
officials. In June 1989, an old and rusted oil pipe releasing gas into
the air exploded near the railway line in the Ural mountains,
killing scores of people. The burning gas continues to spread
dangerous chemicals over many kilometres, poisoning the
atmosphere.

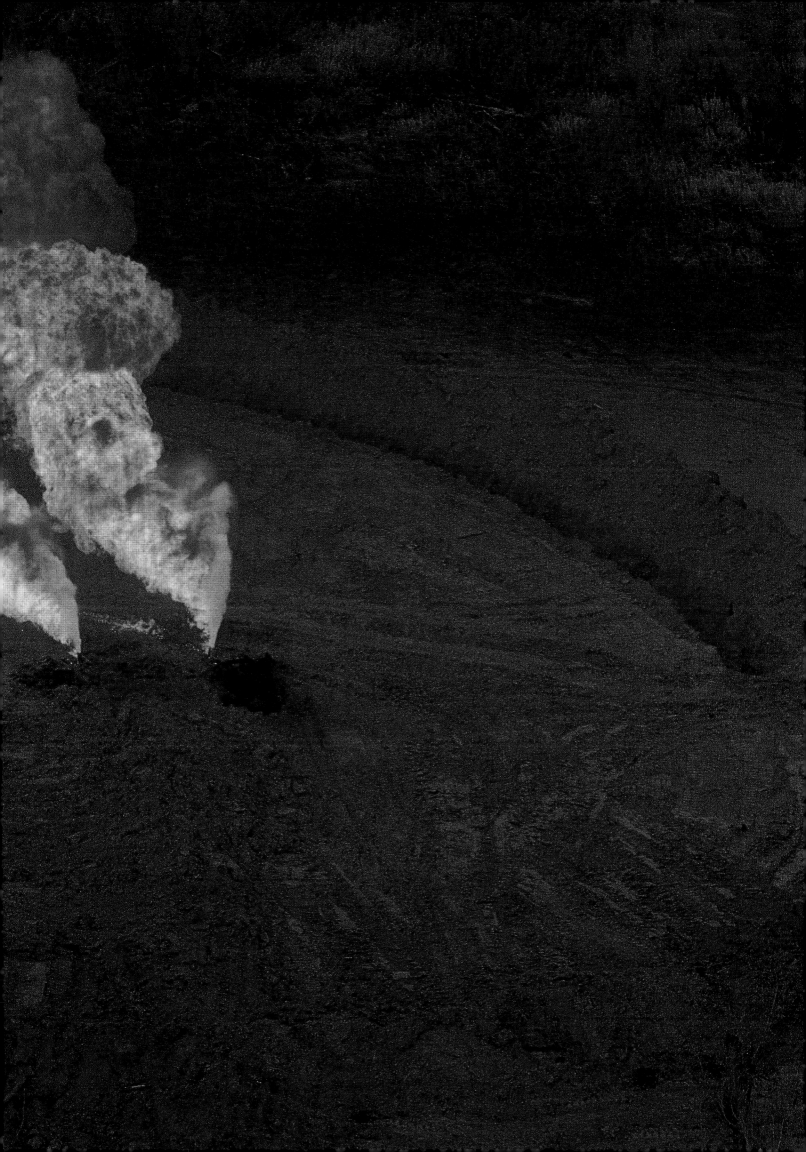

famous Siberian forest, the *Taiga*, only to find a forest of dead trees. And further to the north, on the fragile Yamal Peninsula, some six million hectares of arctic tundra has been laid waste by the oil and gas industry.

"There are lots of accidents," admits one thick-faced drill operator. "Especially now, the large pipelines just break up — they are all very old. Before, if the pipeline broke it would be like a tragedy, all the superiors would come and have a look. But nowadays, they don't seem to notice it."

From another oil rig, Baudi Shoukhaloz looks sadly across a landscape that resembles a battlefield of the apocalypse. In the distance, huge flames rise, topped by billowing clouds of black smoke. Gas is being burnt-off, wasted, because the industry can't get organised to seal it off or tap it. The forest has been denuded. There is no grass. Everywhere there are pools of black oil.

"We're all unhappy, me and the rest. We get together quite often after work and we talk about these problems all the time. It's a pity of course that such things are happening here, in some of the most beautiful places. Surely, we destroyed them.

"My son and I went fishing," Baudi continued. "We didn't catch any fish. My kid is very little. He asked, 'Why haven't we caught anything?' He couldn't understand and I couldn't explain it to him. So we left. How could I answer him? That there are wells there, and that there are spills or something else? If I explained that he'd ask, 'But why are they there?' I can't explain it all to him. I know there will be a time when we're all condemned and my son will say: 'You made all this mess!' In the future this nature that was destroyed, it will be blamed on us."

On the Trans-Siberian, such problems can't be seen by the ordinary traveller. Day three, and my "conversations" with

An aerial view of rural workers in a field near Tyumen. Not everyone works in the oilfields.

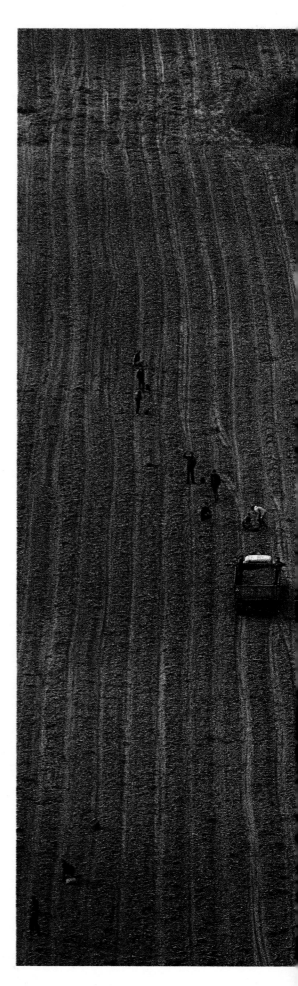

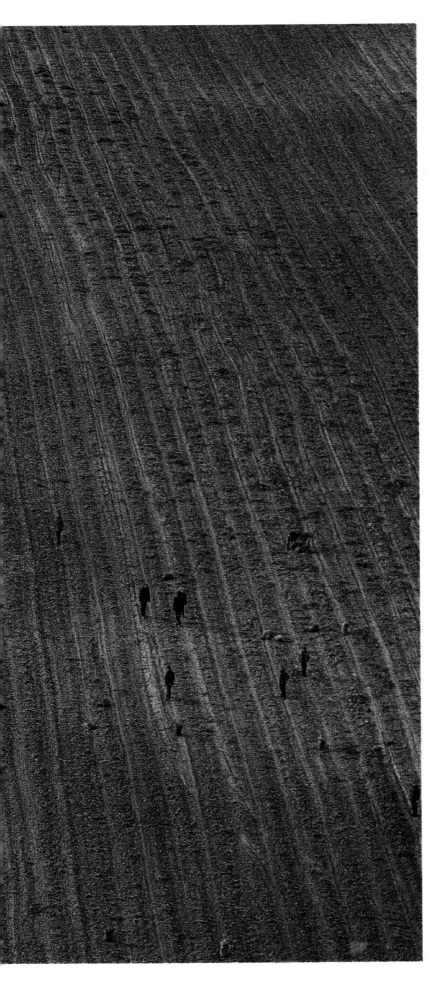

Boris and Misha turned, as all conversations in the Soviet Union seemed to do, to money. Music may be an international language, but money seems as easily understood and certainly more popular. A pen, notebook and exchange rate are all that's needed to get to the very fundamentals of existence. Soon my notebook was groaning with Boris and Misha's calculations: How much money did I make a month? How expensive was my house? What was my car worth? After each scribbled calculation they would sit back and shake their heads in disbelief. As I asked the same questions of them, the whole exercise became more and more uncomfortable. For despite the absurdity of direct comparisons, there was a certain poignancy in the fact that my very average car was worth a lifetime's wage in roubles. I tried to introduce some perspective by pointing out that while half my income was consumed by a home mortgage, they paid a mere ten per cent of their incomes for a subsidised government flat. Furthermore, I implored, an average meal in the Soviet Union was far cheaper, in relative terms, than in the West. They weren't convinced.

Misha dismissively waved his hand at the food on the table and a drawing of his flat, then spat. "What good is cheap food when there's little food to buy?" he seemed to be saying. "What joy in a cheap flat if you don't want to live there?" Their obsessive questioning only seemed to confirm what they already knew, that their standard of living wasn't anywhere near that in the West.

The discomfort was relieved when the train pulled up for one of its two or three daily stops, only a half-day now from Novosibirsk. I always felt like a dog being let out of its kennel as I bounded off the train and into the crisp, but gloriously fresh air. Beside me, three young girls from the Novosibirsk ballet school stretched their long legs. But for

the smokers, a category which takes in most Russian men, it was a chance to puff away in dignity rather than huddle in the crowded vestibules at the end of each carriage where the smoke is sometimes so thick lighting-up seems a waste of time. The brief stops are also a chance to supplement the stringy chicken and oily borsch which passes for cuisine on the train, though the boiled potatoes and pickled gherkins sold by squat peasant women for a few *kopecks*, soon lose their novelty.

Lenin described the West Siberian steppe as "extraordinarily featureless", but as the *Rossiya* slogged on and on towards Novosibirsk, its very sameness gave it a hypnotic fascination. There is not the smallest rise to disturb the flatness, and as far as the eye could see was nothing but an endless patchwork of open grass plains, randomly broken by copses of birch and aspen, only to give way to grass again. Occasionally, in the middle of this loneliness, was a single house buffeted by a bitter wind. You could sleep or read for hours, only to look up and find that nothing had changed. For hundreds and hundreds of kilometres in every direction the steppe stretches. I imagined walking off into it, away from the train, deeper and deeper into the great silence, and finally arriving at the edge of the world. And lording above all this stretched a vast, silent sky which made oneself, the train, even the steppe, seem small and unimportant.

Then suddenly, the world intrudes as a freight train flashes past in the opposite direction, rattling the windows of the carriage as it thunders by. The romantic image of the Trans-Siberian as a single train heroically inching across the curve of the globe is, unfortunately, a myth. At any one time there are fourteen *Rossiyas* carrying ten thousand people from Moscow to Vladivostok and back. Then there are the scores of passenger trains ploughing shorter routes across Siberia.

But most frequent of all are the freight trains. The Soviet rail system carries more freight traffic than any in the world and its busiest line is the Trans-Siberian. At times the trains pass every few minutes, some so long they take almost a minute to pass, groaning with immense loads of logs, farm machinery, cars, containers from Japan or military equipment. Sometimes it's difficult to see the wood for the trains.

Quite abruptly the steppe finished, the train now running past hundreds of small *dachas*, the tiny country shacks with their small gardens, ownership of which is a popular dream for all Russians. A little further on a large group of Gypsies had set up camp by the tracks, washing hanging from lines, small fires smoking beside colourful canvas tents. There are two hundred thousand Gypsies in the Soviet Union and they retain their Indian features, their dialect, and their instinct for wandering.

The train slowed as it dipped into a river valley and across a large bridge. Three thousand, three hundred and forty three kilometres from Moscow, we were crossing one of the world's longest rivers, the Ob. On the other side was Novosibirsk, the largest city in Siberia and seventh largest in the empire. As the train pulled up, I said goodbye to Boris and Misha, and in the warm handshakes realised how strong a bond three days of knocking knees and breaking bread had created. They presented me with a can of Russian fishpaste as a memento of the journey. I couldn't bring myself to throw it out for a month afterwards.

Novosibirsk is called the Chicago of Siberia, but the only similarity I could ascertain between the two cities was the bitterly cold wind. It is a city born of the Trans-Siberian, and with a dual role as a major river port on the Ob, it has developed into Siberia's largest industrial centre with steel, engineering and chemical industries providing

Houses like these sprang up in the late nineteenth century, a time of prosperity for Tyumen. Already an important trade centre, it was the first to be connected to the Siberian railway. Most of these houses with the ornamented window frames that Tyumen became famous for were commissioned by well-to-do merchants who wanted the first Siberian city (it was founded in 1508) to equal St Petersburg and Moscow. Today each of these buildings houses a number of families. They lack basic facilities like water and heating, and are largely in disrepair.

Left: *A Gypsy girl. Gypsies do not fit comfortably into the Soviet system. Their nomadic tradition contradicts the spirit of* propiska, *which means that every citizen has an officially registered place of residence, and being found anywhere else for a suspiciously long period of time is a criminal offence. The Gypsy habits have prompted various laws and decrees after the revolution, eventually inducing them to a settled way of life. But they seem to circumvent this problem at least some of the time, when in the summer months entire communities take off and travel for whatever reason they find suitable, trading being one of them.* Top: *A railway workers' outpost in the Novosibirsk region.* Below: *The long train journey provides plenty of time for children to play and enjoy each other's company, while adults sleep.*

Approaching Novosibirsk, the bridge on the River Ob is the longest on the Trans-Siberian. Completed in the 1980s, it replaced the older bridge behind it which was completed in 1893. The Ob, some 2 kilometres wide at this point, is a major tranport route for barges and river shipping.

employment for the city's one and a half million people. Many Soviet industries shifted east of the Urals to safety during the Second World War. Three hundred thousand workers were relocated to Novosibirsk with their factories and most remained here. In 1961, the Soviet Academy of Sciences opened a Siberian branch, creating an academic town (Akademgorodok) and university just to the south of the city. Some forty thousand scientists and their families have moved to Akademgorodok since it was founded, making it one of the most important research centres in the Soviet Union. Built amongst a forest of pine trees, devoid of any factories, it is the antithesis to industrial Novosibirsk, and those that live there see it as a sanctuary.

My guide was a young Russian – English translator called Philipov, who lived and worked in Akademgorodok. As he showed me around the grounds of the town's university it struck me how different it was to any campus I'd seen in the West. There was no graffiti here, no posters on the walls, no loud rabble of students, no youthful eccentricity, just a dull collection of buildings surrounded by a strange quiet. As we talked about Gorbachev's reforms, and the Soviet Union's slow shift towards democracy, I expected Philipov to be enthused and excited, but he displayed the negativity and cynicism of a disgruntled old man.

"Russians will always be doomed to serfdom of one form or another," he said. "Democracy will never come here, maybe democracy doesn't even suit our people. Life goes on. I hold no faith in politicians. Nothing will change."

I had come across a surprising number of people who shared the same view, believing Russia's history had a complete monopoly over its future. Some told me they believed it was a psychological trait of the Russian people to acquiesce to authoritarian rule and tyranny. Democracy might be fine for the

Train station art: a peace salute at Novosibirsk Railway Station.

"intellectuals", they said, but for the "ordinary" people it was an irrelevant and useless concept. To someone brought up to cherish democracy, I found the argument as backward as the Luddites'. It patronised the vast majority of Russians by assuming they didn't possess even the simple commonsense to know what was best for them or their country and, like children, required a big brother with a big stick. It irritated me, but I heard the same argument from so many people that it left a nagging uncertainty in the back of my mind. I was never totally convinced they were wrong.

Like all cities which are under snow for much of the year, Novosibirsk swirls with dust and grit after the spring thaw. There are few old buildings, few that are beautiful, and it seems an incongruous place for one of the Soviet Union's most famous ballet schools, the Novosibirsk State School of Choreography. It occupies an unremarkable building, but produces some of the best dancers in the country. With a hundred and fifty students from across Siberia, the best will go to Leningrad or Moscow, with the very best joining the Bolshoi Ballet.

A day after arriving, I took a taxi to Iskitim, a small, non-descript town 50 kilometres from Novosibirsk at the end of a pot-holed road. Iskitim has no claim to fame, but a strong one to infamy. From 1933 to 1956, it was the site of one of the Soviet Union's most notorious labour camps, part of what Alexander Solzhenitsyn described as the "Gulag archipelago". Along with common criminals, Stalin sent millions of political prisoners to the Gulag, creating a vast workforce of cheap slave labour which became the backbone of many Soviet export industries. Pathologically suspicious, he eliminated not only his real enemies, but anyone he didn't like. Prisoners dug canals, laid roads and railroads, farmed, mined. Even now, in

Above: *A dance lesson at the Novosibirsk State School of Choreography.*
Right: *1st September. The first day of school in Russia has long been cultivated as a day full of social and ideological significance for the "young citizens". Bright flowers adorn school uniforms to create just the right combination of seriousness and celebration. After the traditional welcoming speeches the children are marched to their classrooms where they will spend the next eleven years.*

central Novosibirsk, there are construction sites surrounded by wooden fences and watchtowers where prisoners toil only a few metres from passers-by. In Stalin's time, however, the convict workforce was expendable. Along with executions, it has been estimated by some that over twenty million people died as a direct result of Stalin's tyranny, as many as were killed during the war. At the height of the Great Terror, in the late 1930s, the Soviet Union was a nation where virtually half the population were prisoners, and the other half gaolers. This from a man who once said: "There is nothing more precious in the world than man himself."

At Iskitim, the exiles mined limestone for cement and on the town's outskirts it is still possible to see the barbed wire and tumbledown walls of the camp barracks beside the quarry, now full of water. There was once a sign above its gates which read: "Labour is a matter of honour, courage and heroism." It was little different from the sign I'd seen above Auschwitz: "Work will make you free." And like Auschwitz, the only real freedom was in death. Most people sent to Iskitim died a slow death from the limestone dust that choked the air and burnt their lungs. A guide from the local memorial society put it bluntly: "It was a camp for the condemned. It meant death."

Iosif Shelkovsky is one of the few survivors of Iskitim. An arthritic man in his seventies, he now lives a short distance away with his wife Katerina. He spent ten years in Iskitim for making a disparaging aside about Stalin, surviving only because he was a builder whose skills kept him working away from the limestone pit. Normally a silent man, he suddenly bursts forth in a loud and sudden anger when he talks of the past.

"I was on the Polish front and I was arrested because I said Stalin 'wasn't a soldier, but an amateur'. It's true and I'll say it again. He wasn't a soldier, he was a scoundrel and a rogue. He was a scoundrel who put down as many people as the war did."

Shelkovsky described how work began before dawn and finished after dark. Hunger was a weapon. Each day's ration depended on fulfilling a work quota, but with meagre rations the less you ate, the less you were able to produce. Thieves and thugs amongst the criminals stole food from the politicals. Then there was the brutality of the camp commanders. He abruptly recounted an incident that had long festered in his mind. It happened one evening. The commander was demanding reports on the day's work.

"'Shelkovsky! How much have you accomplished?' 'Two hundred and fifty per cent sir!' 'Go right through.' 'Petrovsky, how much have you accomplished?' 'Sir, how can we talk about accomplishments when people can hardly stand?'"

"And then," Shelkovsky paused and shook his head, "he shot him right between the eyes. Bang. Bang. Bang. Shot in the head and he's dead."

He sighed and leant back in his chair. "Ah, I don't want to remember. I dream about all the sorrow. When you forget it's easier on your soul."

"Stalin wasn't a soldier, he was a scoundrel and a rogue." The price Iosif Viktorovich Shelkovsky paid for making a small jibe about Stalin while a foot soldier on the Polish Front was ten years in a Siberian labour camp. Part of the "Gulag Archipeligo", the camp at Iskitim was amongst the most notorious in the country. Many people died working in the limestone pit where the dust ate away their lungs. As a building engineer, Iosif was able to avoid working where many of his friends perished. "It's true what I said, and now I'll say it again. Stalin was a rogue who killed as many people as the war did."

CHAPTER FIVE

COMING IN FROM THE COLD

Novosibirsk to Vladivostok

The Trans-Siberian is hell on earth to some, but to railway buffs it is the kingdom of heaven. A day out of Novosibirsk and Basil Tellwright FCIT, MCIM, M.Inst.T.A., was looking dreamily out the window at the endless expanse of Siberian Steppe.

"You know," he said, pausing to signal the pronouncement of a Great Truth. "Here the car doesn't count, there's no highway across Siberia. It's just the railway. The railway is king."

I thought Basil was about to stand to attention and bellow "Long live the king!" down the corridors of the train, but he contained himself. Of course, what he'd said was perfectly true. Siberia is one of the few places in the world where the train hasn't been upstaged or conquered by the automobile. There are no bus tours across Siberia, no semi-trailers carrying freight, no smog; just four ribbons of metal with a tireless stream of trains shuttling back and forth like caterpillars on a branch.

Basil belonged to a group of fourteen English rail buffs, or more precisely a group of seven English rail buffs — all retired employees of Brit Rail — who had shanghaied their wives into travelling by train from London to Hong Kong. It had begun badly — a railway strike in Holland had reduced them to the ignominy of travelling by bus to Berlin, but now they were happy as pigs in swill.

There are few people quite so eccentric as rail buffs. Anyone who can

Winter in Siberia. As the carriages of the Trans-Siberian move into the region known as Zabaikalie (the land beyond the lake), temperatures can drop to below minus-thirty degrees Celsius. Birch and pines are the most common trees throughout the journey.

Above: *Provodniks are probably less enthusiastic about the food served on Soviet trains than anyone else, because they have to eat it more often. The dish is* bifshtex, *derivative of the English word beef-steaks, but there the similarity ends. Meat, mash, peas and gravy is more accurate.*
Right: *The Trans-Siberian is a long journey, and sleep is one way to shorten it.*

sit for hours in their lounge room listening to a recording of the whooshes and whistles of the *Flying Scotsman* travelling from London to Edinburgh, going into ecstasy when it strains on a hill, must qualify as a little strange. My English friends were no exception. One of their group could judge the precise speed of the train by calculating the number of clunk-clunks per second as the wheels went over the joins in the track. I'd never had a discussion about the coupling systems of trains, but having done so for an hour, I can report that the excessive clanking of Soviet trains when they stop and start is the result of technology improved on in other countries fifty years ago.

Some of the technological shortcomings of the Soviet rail network were confirmed in a brief conversation I later had with a driver on the Trans-Siberian who was changing shifts at one of the stops. He was proud of his job being in charge of the country's number one train, the *Rossiya*, but distressed at the state of the Czechoslovakian engine that was pulling it.

"Look at this locomotive," he said. "It should have been written-off ages ago, twenty years ago. But it'll be on the tracks for another twenty years."

It is a two day, two night trip from Novosibirsk to Irkutsk, and by now I was discovering that the longest train journey in the world *is* the longest train journey in the world. The six hundred passengers on the *Rossiya* drifted into a trance-like state which made me think the provodniks were slipping tranquillisers in the tea. It was the land of the living dead. Robust Russian men and women lay slumped on their bunks like beached whales waiting to be pushed back into the sea. Limbs went limp, eyes glazed over, people wandered up and down the corridors in dressing-gowns and dishevelled clothes like sleep-walkers. Conversation slowed and

eventually ground to a halt. Even reading became boring. I found myself staring out the window with the unfocused eyes of the lobotomised, because what's the sense of focusing on anything if everything is the same? Somehow, I even became oblivious to the discordant symphony of smells which wafted around my head in the stale air. Only the olfactory assault of venturing into the toilets — the ones nearest the provodniks' cabin are always the cleanest — stirred the brain-dead follicles in my nose. I decided to re-categorise "the world's greatest train journey" once again. It had already slipped from romance to adventure. Now it was just plain experience.

But after a few days on the Trans-Siberian none of this seems to matter. Even time becomes unimportant. You eat when you are hungry, sleep when you are tired. Clock time becomes meaningless because the train takes no notice of the eight time zones it passes through on the way to Vladivostok, but keeps to Moscow time for the entire journey. I took off my watch, irritated by the absurdity of eating breakfast at midnight and going to sleep in darkness in the mid-afternoon. The train was a limbo land where hours have little meaning, minutes are irrelevant and seconds are a waste of time.

The real world intruded when the train arrived at Krasnoyarsk, a busy industrial city of nearly a million people on the Yenisey River, roughly half-way between Novosibirsk and Irkutsk. Basil and his friends bounded out of the train highly excited by a display of fly-shunting, where goods carriages are pushed up a small incline and left to career, apparently out of control, into various sidings. The joy on their faces was tempered by excruciating frustration, because none of this they were allowed to film. In fact, their Intourist guide had told them they were not allowed to take any photos, not only of military hardware, but of trains, bridges, tunnels and railway platforms for "security reasons". For the rail buffs, cameras still slung uselessly over their shoulders, their angst was made all the worse when I told them we had been given almost unlimited access to film the Soviet rail system for the book and documentaries. Someone had forgotten to tell their guide the Cold War had eased. It was typical of the absurd inconsistencies of Soviet bureacracy which, earlier on, had allowed me into Lithuania when the border was officially "closed". Basil was highly unimpressed.

I walked up to the end of the platform where a small gang of railway workers in bright orange jackets were checking points on the lines. Nearly four million workers are employed in the Soviet rail network and it is common to see gangs of fettlers standing by the tracks waiting for the train to pass before they can resume work. Among them are a surprising number of women, reflecting the high percentage of women who work in jobs normally the domain of men in the West. The war and Stalin's purges have left the Soviet Union with twenty million less men than women and one senses the high number of women occupying traditionally male positions is more the result of necessity, rather than an enlightened policy of equal opportunity between the sexes.

In the small group at Krasnoyarsk Station a young woman called Larissa was heaving on the end of a large sledge-hammer. She had worked as a track fitter for five years since leaving school at sixteen, forced to abandon her studies as a pastry cook when she fell pregnant and had to go out and work to support her child. Both her parents had worked on the railroads before her and had paid dearly. Her father lost his health, her mother lost a shoulder and an arm when

Washing dishes on the world's longest train journey may not be the world's greatest job, but this Russian woman hasn't let it get her down.

175

Larissa Lonzhuk is twenty-two, a railway worker at Krasnoyarsk Station. There are many women doing hard manual labour on the Soviet railways, but you won't find a woman driving a train. Despite socialism's rhetoric of equal rights, women have only been given the right to work as physically hard as men. They rarely occupy positions of power and still they are expected to do "women's" work at home.

176

she was run over by a train in a snow storm. There was little about her work that she liked.

"Everything makes it difficult," she said. "You've got to carry tools around like this. It weighs eighty kilos. Try and carry that around all day long. We work with diesel oil and scrape the railway points. Our sleeves are soiled, our vests are soiled, our pants are soiled. People look down on you. We stand in the queue in the dining room and we're all dirty. Everybody keeps away from you. Work is hard for women. I think the railways is no place for women. Because there's your health, too. You give your life away and who needs you afterwards? They won't even remember you."

For all the socialist realist posters heroically depicting women side by side with men, heaving the wheels of industry and tilling the fields, the lot of women in the Soviet Union is little advanced. Under Soviet law men and women have equal rights, but while many sexual stereotypes have been broken down, it is still a society dominated by men with few women occupying positions of influence. Women account for fifty-one per cent of the workforce, but their average wage is only sixty-five per cent of the average male wage, reflecting the lower positions they hold. And virtually no women have succeeded in penetrating the top echelons of power in the Communist Party. Aside from the limitations on career advancement, there is an added insult. For as well as doing men's work, they are still expected to do women's work when they get home; run the house, cook the meal, look after the family.

There are also other tyrannies for women. The main form of contraception in the Soviet Union is abortion, with many women having an average of six or more abortions in their lifetime. Few Soviet women have access to the pill,

In Soviet Socialist Realist art women were heroically depicted heaving the wheels of industry and tilling the fields. Many women now work in heavy labouring jobs normally the domain of men in the West, partly because the male workforce was decimated during the war and at the hands of Stalin. But while many sexual stereotypes have been broken down, sexism is still rampant.

and there is little, if any, sex education in schools. Debates on prostitution and homosexuality, both illegal, are often reactionary and conservative, while newspapers even prudishly baulk at referring to condoms. The implications of such attitudes in the battle against AIDS is frightening.

While the West may be guilty of flaunting sex for profit, until recently there was little in official Soviet culture which indicated sex even existed. There are few nudes in Soviet art, erotic films didn't exist, and Soviet fashion seemed desperate to hide bodies rather than show them off. "IN THE SOVIET UNION THERE IS NO SUCH THING AS SEX" read a button on sale at Izmailovsky Park, in Moscow. But with glasnost there have been some changes; television soaps allude to sex and even allow the occasional nude scene, magazines are beginning to publish erotic pictures, sex manuals are available at bookstalls. And as feminists around the world are trying to destroy the portrayal of women as sex objects, in the Soviet Union there is a sudden burgeoning of fashion parades and beauty contests. Some see it as reclaiming a lost "femininity".

"After the revolution women became work-horses and gave all their lives for the building of socialism and communism," says Marina Goldovskaya, a Soviet film-maker who has won international awards for her documentary films. "I was never taught to think of myself as being a woman. I was a member of society but the sexual belonging was ignored. Our society ignored this question. It absolutely ignored mateship. You see it was an indoctrinated society. It was not fair on quite normal human needs. It was utopic, and that's why people lost their sexual belonging. Now, during the Gorbachev years, there is an attempt to give back to women their women-like features. That's why on TV we can now see very sexy

women, so it is an attempt I think to return women to a normal position in this society. Because a woman is a woman, and a man is a man."

This rural scene could be anywhere in the countryside of the Soviet Union.

Just as the train left Krasnoyarsk Station an Intourist "information" tape started up, and in the stilted English common to such things, began a running commentary on the journey to Irkutsk. Crossing the kilometre-long bridge over the Yenisey River, I discovered the huge piers supporting it were built to withstand huge blocks of ice that flow down the river in spring like out of control barges. Constructed in the 1890s the bridge contained "many tonnes of concrete shipped from St Petersburg and steel bearings from Warsaw". Next was a laboriously detailed account of the industrial successes of Krasnoyarsk, followed by mention of the fact we would soon be travelling through the valleys and mountains of the Sayan Range, leaving behind the flatness of the steppe.

But it wasn't long before the tape made a wide detour of geography and launched into some spirited propaganda in support of Gorbachev and perestroika. It was a relentless recitation of figures and forecasts, with a promise that Soviet citizens would reap the benefits of restructuring by the early 1990s. It was like those speeches made by incumbent politicians at election time. Nothing was actually wrong with the country, but everything was going to be much better. Promises masqueraded as certainties. Policies sounded a bit too good and a bit too simple. I imagined the tape as part of a long history of tapes, books, posters and films that have dutifully supported the leaders of the day and their economic initiatives since the revolution. They had sung the praises of collectivisation, of five-year plans, of seven-year plans, of fifteen-year plans, of virgin lands campaigns, of maize

Lenin is ubiquitous, even in the middle of Siberia, such as on this hillside outside Irkutsk.

With their painted shutters and detailed fretwork, traditional
Russian houses are still common throughout the country, though many
are falling into disrepair like this one in Irkutsk. Rather than modify a
traditional design, modern Soviet housing is almost entirely in the form
of identical apartment blocks. They are cheap to build, but soulless.

campaigns, and a hundred other campaigns, plans, reforms and initiatives. Some had mild success, many had completely failed, but none matched their promises. Looking out the window at the poverty of passing villages I thought of the millions of Soviet citizens who had already cynically dismissed perestroika as just another failed promise. Glasnost had clearly worked, but I wondered whether perestroika would take a place in world history as the reform which promised most, but delivered least.

As I stepped off the train in Irkutsk, a tall man with a shock of dark hair and wearing broken glasses bounded up, almost knocking me backwards off my feet. He bowed down and with a theatrical sweep of his hand introduced himself as Valentin, my "translator and guide". He was a curious, fidgety man who seemed totally incapable of keeping still, and when he walked it was with fast, agitated little hops that had me half running to keep up with him. I had found him through a friend of a friend of a friend, but was never able to discover exactly what his occupation was. He described himself as a "translator of various publications", but went curiously vague when I sought further details, something made all the more mysterious by the fact that he lived in a town near Irkutsk which was off-limits to foreigners. Most bizarre was the way he spoke, a precise but totally inappropriate English which made him sound like he was reading from a technical journal.

"In relation to your schedule I have made a number of plans and contingencies," said Valentin as he bounced ahead of me along the platform. "You are no doubt fully cognisant of the fact that Irkutsk has been called historically, 'the Paris of Siberia'. I propose that we investigate this reality by first taking in a *visage* of the city. If this course of action is approved by you, then we shall proceed with the first activity."

I gave due approval and so began a punishing schedule which didn't abate.

Irkutsk sits on the eastern bank of the Angara River, a broad and powerful body of water which flows from enormous Lake Baikal just to the east. Throughout the eighteenth and nineteenth centuries the city established itself as the financial and administrative capital of Eastern Siberia. It was a major trading centre for furs and an important stop along the great caravan route bringing tea, silk and porcelain from China. With a gold rush in the early 1800s Irkutsk became a Russian Klondike, and as a growing centre for political or criminal exiles, took on a certain wildness. At the turn of the century there were said to be four hundred murders a year in a town of just 50,000 people, prompting a guidebook of the time to advise "walking in the middle of the road is to court attack from the garrotters with which Siberian towns abound". Among the most celebrated exiles were the Decembrists, a group of noblemen who attempted a coup against the Czar in 1825 and whose wives followed them to Irkutsk. In 1903, Stalin himself was exiled to the city, as were fellow Marxists Dzerzhinsky, Kirov and Molotov.

While Irkutsk bears almost no resemblance to Paris, it is amongst the most beautiful cities in Siberia, simply because many of the old buildings have been preserved. There are still the old brick mansions of the town's wealthy merchants, and the more typical log houses, some two hundred years old, with their detailed fretwork and shutters painted blue or green.

Valentin bounced ahead of me along Karl Marx Street (every Soviet city has one) and in quick succession we passed the opera house, Lenin's statue, the hotel Chekhov stayed in when he passed through Irkutsk in 1890, and a queue of people buying gold in fear of the rouble collapsing further than it had already done. In his precise, scientific tone he piled detail on detail about the city's history, but it was only when I asked about Valentin Rasputin, a well-known Russian writer who lives in Irkutsk, that he got truly excited. A patriot and nationalist, Rasputin is a favourite writer of the Pamyats, a conservative, but widely supported movement which claims to want to instil in Russians a love for their traditional culture (Pamyat means memory), but spends most of its time inciting hatred of the Jews. I asked him what he thought of the Pamyats.

"The Jews have too much control," he said. "It is not natural. They were instrumental in this revolution of ours that was a disaster, and now they occupy too many important positions in society. They take all the positions in universities. It's not a question of blood, it is a question of the mind. The Jews are not for Russia, they are for themselves. It is simply not natural."

I had heard the arguments of the Pamyats in Novosibirsk, where each Sunday large groups of people gather in the local park engaging in spirited debates on everything from democracy to the environment. It was a healthy exercise, one not possible just a few years ago, but of all the groups, the Pamyats stood out as being rabid, aggressive and at times quite frightening. Most horrifying was the sight of adolescent boys in black shirts, with brutally short haircuts wearing swastikas on their chests. In crazed tones they railed on and on about the "Jewish problem" and "cosmopolitans", the liberals who sympathise with the Jews.

"In the year 2000 they will rule the world," yelled one Pamyat supporter. "This is no joke. Sixty-five per cent of

Irkutsk is famous for its history of exiles. Amongst the best known were the Decembrists, a group of noblemen who launched a failed coup against the Czar in 1825. Those that weren't executed, were exiled to Siberia, where their wives followed them. Hardly a life of hardship, this was the residence of a Russian prince, exiled with his wife . . . and his wealth.

In public parks throughout the Soviet Union ideas and issues are now freely debated. Democracy and economic reform are the most common issues, but this group listens to a speaker from an extreme nationalist group, the Pamyats, who blame the country's woes on a traditional scapegoat, the Jews. Anti-semitism is on the rise in the Soviet Union, an ugly phenomenom which is forcing many Jews to leave the country.

187

gold is in their hands. The newspapers of the world are in their hands. This will continue for as long as it takes our people to wake up."

The Pamyats argue that Jews organised the Bolshevik revolution and masterminded Stalin's terror. They see glasnost and perestroika as a conspiracy to allow Jewish capitalists to regain control of the country. Even democracy is a plot of the Zionist mafia. In fact, few Jews were involved in the Bolshevik revolution, and since then virtually none have been admitted into the party's privileged bureaucracy, the *nomenklatura,* particularly the Central Committee. And rather than favouritism, Jews have faced constant discrimination in every aspect of life from education, to jobs and religion. Hebrew was a forbidden language until recently. Yiddish was not taught in schools. There were no institutions to train new Rabbis.

I couldn't understand Valentin. Everything he went on about seemed an absurd and phantom problem. The economy was tumbling down around his head, the empire was being torn apart, and here were the Pamyats blaming the Jews, 1.5 million people in a population of nearly 300 million. Perhaps it was little different to the hatred whipped up against the Jews in the chaos of Weimar Germany. I told him the whole argument didn't make sense to me, especially the implication at the heart of Pamyat philosophy that Jews aren't patriotic, that they don't care about their country.

"They have unnatural control," he mumbled. "It is just not natural."

We didn't broach the subject after that, but from then on Valentin and I regarded each other with suspicion.

That night we drove in darkness to Lake Baikal, 60 kilometres south of Irkutsk, where some friends of Valentin lived in a small *izbah* by the lake. When I woke the next morning and stepped

On the shores of Lake Baikal, the largest reservoir of fresh water in the world, a pulp and paper mill is wreaking havoc. Containing an astounding twenty per cent of the world's total fresh water supply, dioxins and pollutants from the mill and other industries are decimating the lake's unique wildlife and polluting its pristine splendour. While the environmental movement is well behind that of the West, many people have mobilised to save the lake.

189

outside, I was met by one of those sights which is imprinted forever in your memory. Before me was a vast sheet of white, the frozen surface of Lake Baikal, and way, way in the distance, almost imperceptible through the glare and light mist, were the lines of a mountain range on the opposite shore. There was a slight breeze, ice cold, but not a single noise. It was one of those scenes where nature dwarfs humans. Even the small fleet of boats at a nearby dock was helplessly caught in the grip of the ice waiting for the spring thaw.

Lake Baikal is 640 kilometres long, up to 80 kilometres wide and covers an area roughly a quarter the size of England. Beneath the ice, the lake plunges to depths of over 1.5 kilometres. It is the largest reservoir of fresh water on earth, and holds a staggering twenty per cent of the world's total supply, threatened now by a pulp mill and heavy industry on the lake's southern shores. Its sheer size made it one of the most difficult obstacles for the Trans-Siberian, and before construction of the Circumbaikal line, a ferry carried rolling stock and passengers from one shore to the other.

The Buryat people, a local tribe descended from Mongol stock, called the lake bai-kul, or "Rich Lake". Some five hundred plants and 1,200 animals have been identified in and around it, two-thirds of which are found nowhere else. The most unusual inhabitants are a colony of nerpas or Arctic seals, (normally a salt-water animal), which are thought to have migrated from the Arctic Circle up the Yenisey and Angara Rivers. The omul and the sturgeon are the most commonly caught fish, with sturgeon weighing up to 200 kilograms and capable of producing 8 kilograms of caviar. Despite temperatures of minus thirty degrees Celsius and ice up to 3 metres thick, fishing still continues throughout winter in Siberia. It is an elaborate, painstaking affair. Boats are

Top Left: *Lake Baikal is one of the Soviet Union's environmental treasures. "Baikal" means "rich lake" in the Buryat language. It is home to hundreds of plant and animal species not found anywhere else.* **Left:** *These Buryat horsemen from the village of Ranzburovo work on a collective farm, breeding cattle and animals for fur. The Buryats are famous for their horsemanship as these men, proudly dressed in their traditional costume, are happy to demonstrate. Ethnic culture in Soviet society has long been suppressed, despite the facade of displays like this.* **Above:** *A Buryat child. With growing nationalism and self-determination sweeping the Soviet Union, this young boy will grow up to consider himself a Buryat first and a Soviet citizen last.*

The Buryats are one of the largest ethnic groups in the Soviet Union, but like all ethnic minorities they have had to struggle to retain their identity. With their own language and history suppressed by an education system which concentrates on Soviet history and the Russian language, it has been a difficult fight. Nevertheless some traditions survive. A traditional Buryat feast begins with the slaughter of a ram. Nothing is wasted, even the blood is used in sausages.

replaced by horse-drawn sleds, and after digging a series of holes in the ice, the fishermen drop down nets, threading them from one hole to the other before using the horses to haul them from the water.

Stretching eastward from Lake Baikal, the Buryat Autonomous Republic is home to the largest ethnic minority in Siberia. The Buryats were once nomadic, with a strong Mongolian tradition of horsemanship, but eventually settled around Lake Baikal where they took up farming and fishing.

In 1881 the Reverend Henry Lansdell described coming across the Buryat in his book *Through Siberia*. "We first met with these people a few miles on the western side of Irkutsk, and their physiognomy at once told us they belonged to a different race from any we had seen. They have large skulls, square faces, low and flat foreheads; the cheekbones are high and wide apart, the nose flat, eyes elongated, the skin swarthy and yellowish, and the hair jet black."

Despite decades of policies which attempted to forge all ethnic minorities into an all-embracing Soviet identity, the Buryats have retained a strong sense of self. They still proudly trace their ancestry back to Genghis Khan and their religious traditions to Tibetan Buddhism and Shamanism. They speak a language closely related to Mongolian, and in the face of Soviet schooling and Soviet control, many of their customs have survived since the revolution. A traditional Buryat feast is little different today than a century ago. A sheep is slaughtered by cutting a small hole in its chest, reaching in and pinching the aorta. Nothing is wasted. Marrow is sucked from the bones, even the blood is drunk. It's a carnivore's picnic, complete with traditional costume and songs.

"In the past we were oppressed because they pressured us from the top,"

194

In winter, the lakes across Siberia freeze to a depth of up to 2 metres. Despite that, the fishing industry continues. On Lake Kotokel, east of Lake Baikal, local fishermen travel to the middle of the lake by horse and sled, not boats. Nets are lowered through holes cut in the ice, then pulled along under the frozen surface. As the horses winch the catch from the lake the fish are virtually snap frozen in the sub-zero temperatures. On a good day's ice fishing up to a ton of fish, can be pulled from the lake. Last year's record was six tons in a single day, but in years gone by a day's catch could be as much as ten tons.

said a Buryat woman from a small village near Ulan-Ude. "But now I think people should raise themselves even more to preserve the national flavour of our village. People should raise their culture and their ancient customs. That way our Buryat traditions will survive."

It was another three days now from Irkutsk to Vladivostok, skirting the Chinese border much of the way until the Trans-Siberian reached Khabarovsk then headed south for the final run to the Pacific port. I had upgraded my ticket to first class — something which no-one remembered or cared to charge me for — and I was now basking in the comparative luxury of a two bed compartment, better quality linen and the refined touch of a small bunch of flowers on the table. But the most pleasant change was sharing the cabin with an Intourist guide who was accompanying a motley group of English speaking tourists. A young Russian woman in her mid-twenties, she had a charming smile, but everything about her was infused with an air of melancholy. She introduced herself as Olga, and after exchanging pleasantries she asked that dreaded question.

"Well, do you like my country?"

It was the same question Nikita Tolstoy had asked me, and as it hung in the air, I imagined the countless foreigners who rubbed her nose in the problems of the Soviet Union every day. Rich, pampered westerners — some well-meaning, others self-righteous — but all complaining about the food, the accommodation, the service, the rudeness, the delays and the politics. I paused for what seemed an eternity, not wanting to sound like all the others, but after a few moments gushing about the beauty of Lake Baikal, the charms of Irkutsk and the warmth of the people, I heard myself relating the despair I'd felt in Leningrad and Moscow.

"Everybody says the same," she said. "But it's true. We have many problems. The only difference now is I can talk about how bad things are."

It has long been the job of Intourist guides to sing the praises of their country and play political commissars to the capitalists, but in the age of glasnost, Olga gave me a frank tour of Soviet life in which she had virtually nothing good to say. At an age when most young people are excited by the possibilities of life, she seemed burdened only by the problems. She still lived in a Moscow flat with her mother and could never foresee the day she would be able to move into a flat of her own. She talked about the miseries of standing in queues, how the struggle to find food and clothes had so monopolised people's minds they could talk of nothing else. She spoke fluent French and English, but earned only 180 roubles a month. It was the equivalent of about one US dollar a day, but Intourist charged her services out at a hundred and twenty dollars a day.

"That's what you call capitalism," she said.

After the flat monotony of much of Siberia, the country we travelled through now was interesting at every turn. The railway snaked for hours along the bank of the Ingoda River with a patchwork of broken ice muscling down its course. It passed through a landscape of bald, rolling hills, which never seemed to end. In the yellow light of the afternoon sun, they looked soft, inviting and strangely surreal. I wondered how they would look in winter, when even at these comparatively low latitudes the temperature can fall to minus fifty degrees Celsius. Snow stays on the ground for half the year, and not far to the north begins the permafrost. Occasionally, a small village with just a handful of houses would nestle in a fold of the hills. Nearby would be a small graveyard with turquoise coloured

The Russian folk choir of Chita's railway repair factory singing "Golden Russia", a patriotic song about bare birches, wide open spaces, cranes in flight and the Russian dawn.

Sunset from the train, near Khabarovsk, in the far east of the Soviet Union. In western Russia it is still morning, Moscow is seven hours behind.

Above: *Soldiers from an infantry regiment near Ulan Ude, not far from the Soviet/Chinese border, and one of the coldest regions in Siberia. Driven as much by the need to save a crippled economy as a desire to end superpower tensions, Mikhail Gorbachev has slashed military spending. This regiment was once two thousand men strong, now there are two hundred.* Right: *Soldiers on military exercises.*

crosses, enclosed by a neat fence. On one hillside, in the middle of nowhere, I saw a statue of Lenin looking across this lonely world. People and politics seemed irrelevant in the vastness.

But politics were closer than I imagined. Just 100 kilometres to the south was the border with China, skirting along the Amur River for much of its 2800 kilometre length from Mongolia to the sea of Okhotsk. It is a sensitive military zone, peppered with army bases. While a number of border areas are still in dispute, tensions have reduced in recent years, particularly after Gorbachev's visit to China in 1989, which swept away thirty years of deep mutual suspicion and animosity between the two communist giants. Through Olga I had spoken briefly to a Soviet Major travelling from Chita to Khabarovsk where he was a regiment commander at a base on the Trans-Siberian. He was a formal man from a long-serving military family, who somehow managed to look as crisp after two days' travel as he did when he first got on the train. With Gorbachev's cutbacks in military spending, he said his troop numbers, all young conscripts, had been reduced from two thousand to a mere two hundred soldiers.

"The actual quantity doesn't determine the army's fighting efficiency," he insisted. "The army can be smaller but better trained . . . but generally speaking, cutbacks are something of a stress for the military. Everybody has to restructure and all this stuff affects us morally and physically as well."

With arms reductions, the disintegration of the Warsaw Pact and heavy cuts in military spending over the next few years, there is disorientation and alarm in the Soviet military. Once the pride of the country after defeating Hitler in the "Great Fatherland War", the military now faces a growing chorus of derision and ridicule. With no aggressors

to fight, no countries to invade, they have been reduced to bullying troublesome Soviet republics in their own country. Then there is the shame of a disastrous war in Afghanistan.

"This war was a mistake and indeed the war was illegal," said the Major. "We have said the truth about the war. We shouldn't have interfered in their internal affairs. Now this issue has been basically settled, but of course it's left an imprint. Mostly it's left a mark on those who took part in the war."

I remembered walking past a health clinic on the shores of Lake Baikal and peering inside to see a group of athletic, bare-chested, young men pushing and straining against the strength of their own arms. The building had once been a resort for senior party members, but had since been given over to treating soldiers. The young men were the Soviet equivalent of Vietnam veterans, trying, like the Americans, to come to terms with having fought in a war lost to peasants and farmers, a war which few people supported back home.

The next morning I woke with the provodnik tugging on my toe and the word "Khabarovsk" ringing in my ears. The train hadn't quite arrived, and as I frantically jumped up and started packing, we rumbled onto what I discovered was the longest bridge on the entire railway. Below me, muddy brown, was the Amur River, some 2 kilometres wide at this point and more like a large lake than a river. Barges were ploughing upstream, small passenger ferries plied back and forth and fishermen sat by the banks waiting for a bite. In winter, the scene is entirely different. Cars and trucks shuttle over the frozen river, while the fishermen continue undisturbed by digging holes in the ice. When the train pulled into Khabarovsk Station I had come 8,531 kilometres from Moscow, now seven time zones behind me.

A hang-glider on the banks of the Amur River looks more like one of the Wright brothers than a modern flier. The further east you travel from Moscow, the more easy-going and carefree seems the mood of the people. Few are so carefree, though, that they fly in home-made hang-gliders.

202

Vladivostok, my last stop in the Soviet Union, was less than a thousand kilometres away.

Hugging a series of hills on a bend in the Amur River, Khabarovsk is an attractive city. It seemed the further we went from Moscow, the cities and people lost their dour sombreness and took on a lighter mood. In Khabarovsk there was no more food in the shops and material conditions were as hard, but with a small circus by the river and a wide beach where families strolled on sunny afternoons, the city had a happier air.

Most of the six hundred thousand people in Khabarovsk are from Russian stock, but along the Amur River live another of the Soviet Union's ethnic minorities, the Nanay people. With flat faces and dark skin, their features are remarkably similar to the Eskimos of Northern Canada. Among their strongest voices is Yevdokia Gaier. A Nanay herself, and a doctor of anthropology, she was recently elected as a People's Deputy defeating a well-known Soviet major in an electorate which has traditionally chosen army officers to reflect the region's military importance. A short, stocky, powerhouse of a character, she first came to national attention for her courageous support of Dr Sakharov, the "conscience" of the Soviet Union, before his death. Since then she has championed the rights, not only of the Nanay people, but of all ethnic groups in the Soviet Union.

"It is a very frightening thing when with each new census we lose a number of indigenous groups in our country," she says. "You know they are still on the verge of extinction today; the culture, the language . . . children in our kindergartens don't speak their mother tongue, they learn it as a foreign language. It is important to do everything to preserve languages wherever possible, to revive them and the traditional culture as well."

Yevdokia Gaier, anthropologist and politician (right) and her adopted aunt Tatiana Khodzher, a traditional Nanay craftswoman. It is the first time they have met since Gaier won an election battle to become a People's Deputy in Moscow, representing an electorate which had previously always been represented by army generals.

I was on the final run south now to Vladivostok. The train had left in the afternoon and would travel in darkness along the sensitive border region with China. I walked down to the dining-car and went through the same absurd ritual that took place in almost every restaurant and dining-car I had visited in the Soviet Union. It had ceased to be depressing, in fact, it had become an amusing game. The waiter brought me the menu, a typically impressive tome many pages long. I perused it, taking a deliberately long time to choose. Perhaps I should indulge in the black caviar for entree, and why not a very traditional Chicken Kiev for main course? The waiter returned and despite the pointlessness of the whole exercise, I placed my order. He smiled apologetically.

"Sorry sir," he said, shrugging his shoulders. "Would you like boiled chicken?"

"Any caviar?"

"Boiled chicken!"

"Any Chicken Kiev?"

"Boiled chicken!"

"Anything other than boiled chicken?"

"Boiled chicken!"

Like every other time, I ordered boiled chicken. When the stringy, runt of a bird arrived, even the waiter grinned at how pathetic it was. Why my guidebook had the Russian translations for partridge, hazel-grouse, Duck a L'orange, pork chops, roast beef, soft caviar, green peas, grapes and bananas was a complete mystery to me.

I returned, hungry, to my cabin and got talking to one of my provodniks, a pimply young man named Jenya and I immediately warmed to him when he told me a joke.

"Did you hear the one about the kindergarten?" he asked.

"'OK children,' said the teacher to the class. 'I want you to tell me in what country children have the most to eat.'

'The Soviet Union,' came the chorus.

'Very good!' said the teacher. 'Now I want you to tell me the country where children have the nicest clothes to wear.'

'The Soviet Union,' the children yelled.

'Excellent!' said the teacher. 'Now tell me the best country in the world for young children to grow up in.'

'The Soviet Union,' the children replied once more.

But suddenly young Sergei started crying at the back of the class.

'What's wrong Sergei?' asked the teacher.

'I want to live in the Soviet Union,' he sobbed."

Jenya had all the hallmarks of an angry young man. He hated his job, the system, the "boring" woman in charge of him, everything. He smoked like a chimney, loved aggressive rock music and tarty looking girls. He hated all things Russian and loved all things Western, to the point where I began defending his country, and criticising my own. We spent much of the evening playing a game of draughts, and after I won the first round he presented me with a pen as a trophy. Before he swapped shifts with his supervisor Ludmilla, we agreed to have a final play-off the next morning.

A kindly woman, Ludmilla was of a different generation to Jenya, and the contrast between them intrigued me. Jenya was growing up in the era of Gorbachev, Ludmilla had grown up in the era of Stalin. While they shared the same hardships and were equally critical of the state of their country, their solutions were worlds apart. While Jenya looked for a golden era in the future, with a naive belief in the ways of the West, Ludmilla looked to the past.

"There was more order in the country," she told me, a small tear welling in her eye. "His only fault was there were many repressions. Many

repressions. But that was the only thing. We had order in the country, and we could buy everything in the shops. Now the country is heading toward decline."

The next morning as the train traversed its last 100 kilometres to Vladivostok, Jenya and I finished our draughts tournament. This time he won, and knowing he expected a trophy, I dug deep into my bag and pulled out a small piece of the Berlin Wall. I could imagine no better present, a small symbol of hope that the walls would continue tumbling down in his own country and pave the way for a better life. But as I gave him the gift his mouth dropped with disappointment. He was silent for a moment, then looked down at the pants I was wearing.

"Can you give me your jeans?" he asked. "Is there anything you can sell me?"

The memory of that went with me as I spent a brief day in Vladivostok, a city which managed to exude the raffish, seaside charm of most ports, despite the ubiquitous columns of Soviet apartments that riddled its hills. Vladivostok was established in 1860 as a military fort and the most far-flung outpost of the Russian empire. Its name translates to "rule the East". As the warm-water base of the Soviet Pacific fleet, the city's military importance has never diminished, and with warships crowded in every finger of its harbour, Vladivostok has been a closed city to foreigners until recently. The fact that I could even visit here, drink with Soviet sailors, walk by the docks, represented another small victory in the easing of global military tension. These were the dying days of the Cold War. The walls were coming down in the Soviet Union. The burden of fear was lifting. But my happiness was tempered thinking of Jenya and knowing that a pair of old jeans was still more valuable than a piece of the most famous wall of our time.

Vladivostok, capital of the Soviet Far-East. With its hills and raffish seaside charm, the city has been called the "Soviet San Francisco". Moscow is seven days and almost 10,000 kilometres to the west. The train has travelled a quarter of the globe to get here, crossing the world's last empire. A crucial warm-water port, Vladivostok was a closed city until recently because of its sensitivity as a military base for the Pacific fleet. Now open to foreigners, it signals another thaw in the dying days of the Cold War.

Dancing girls at the Sailors' Cultural Club in Vladivostok. Is this the last hurrah for communism, or will Mikhail Gorbachev deliver Lenin's dream?

CHAPTER SIX

THE LAST KINGDOM

Suifenhe to Beijing

I had crossed five borders travelling from West Berlin to China, and the first and last had been the most startling. The Berlin Wall had divided the same people into rich and poor. The border with China divided two races.

My train was heading from Suifenhe, on the Chinese/Soviet border, to Harbin, capital of Heilongjiang Province in the frozen north of China. Ever since crossing into East Berlin, and on throughout Eastern Europe and the Soviet Union, I felt I had been travelling through a black and white picture. Now, suddenly, there was colour again. In my carriage a group of Chinese men slapped down cards in a loud, playful game. A farmer had a brace of live chickens in a bag. The dining-car was full of a loud rabble of people, tables piled with food. Outside, villages brimmed with drying corn and cabbages, and mounds of sweet potatoes lay on train platforms ready for transport. The images were confusing. I had stepped from a dour land which was discarding tyranny, but had trouble feeding its people. Now, in a country where tyranny reigned, the people before me looked happy and well-fed. As if to underline the contradiction, a handful of Russians were on the same train making a five-day excursion into China buying consumer items unavailable back home. For the Russians, Third World China had become a shopping destination.

I felt both comfortable and alien here. Comfortable, because suddenly there was a buoyant mood and more to eat. Alien, because the Chinese language and

Travelling through temperatures of minus thirty degrees Celsius, icicles commonly form on trains.

In China, food is suddenly more abundant. Agricultural reforms have worked, even if political reform is non-existent. In a country which has known frequent starvation, food takes on a special importance.

its text seemed even more remote than Russian and Cyrillic. In the Soviet Union I could remain relatively anonymous, but here I was immediately picked as a *yang quaizi*, a "foreign devil" or "big nose". Just as I was beginning to think it would be impossible to make contact with any Chinese, a young man came up and surprised me by asking in perfectly good English where I was from. Wa was a TV salesman who studied computers in his spare time. After doing business in Suifenhe he was making the five-hour trip back to Mudanjiang, on the line to Harbin. If the number of television sets in a society is a barometer of people's living standards, then according to Wa, things had never been better.

"Many people, about seventy per cent in the big cities and about half the people in the countryside, have televisions," he said excitedly. "People's living levels have improved much in recent years. In many Chinese families they have colour TVs, and more than five or six bicycles. Our government has done many good things for the Chinese people."

"If things are so good," I asked, "why did the students revolt in Beijing?"

He paused. "Oh, sorry, I can't answer your question, I don't know." Another pause. "In my opinion I don't support the students' campaign." I was trying to find some sign in his eyes to discover whether he was too frightened to answer the question honestly, or whether he really believed what he said.

"I think the students were cheated by a small crowd of people," he continued. "I think most people support the Chinese Government, especially for financial reforms, and political reforms, because they bring about many changes in various respects in China."

"Did you hear that students were killed by the military?" I asked.

"No, no, no. I haven't heard any news."

"In the West, we heard many students were killed by the military," I said.

"No, I don't believe it. In Mudanjiang there were rumours, but they were only rumours. I don't believe it, because I haven't seen. I haven't heard any news of this kind."

I began to think he did believe what he was saying. As a TV salesman, a purveyor of one of the greatest communication tools known to man, his ignorance seemed especially ironic. He appeared to know virtually nothing about the Beijing massacre of June 1989, an event which had dominated world attention like no other massacre before it. Not only did he know very little, he showed no sign of questioning what he did know. As I travelled through northern China, I was constantly surprised that people were either only vaguely aware of the events in Beijing, or had an opinion shaped entirely by the state-run media. For according to Beijing television, "not even one person died" in Tienanmen Square on June 4.

At Mudanjiang I said goodbye to Wa. While the train took on passengers for the trip to Harbin, I was drawn to the massive locomotive steaming and gasping at the front of the train. In 1988 China still had seven thousand steam trains at work, one of the few places in the world where steam locomotives still rule over diesel and electric. I had never had a close look at a steam locomotive before, and I surprised myself with the rush of childish excitement I felt. It was a big black, prehistoric beast, puffing and wheezing, impatient to go. White steam gushed against its black boiler. Coal dust and grime caked its body. Massive red wheels sat there, full of suppressed energy, a slide bar stretched across them like a weightlifter's forearm. The train had an earthy smell of coal and steam. No machine I had ever seen looked so alive. From the tiny cabin perched on the back of the monster, a grubby Chinese

face peered out wearing a small cap. It seemed that the train itself was in charge, and like a jockey on a fiery race horse, the driver was only in control because the beast allowed it. Seeing this creature made me realise why people get teary eyed when they remember the steam age. I thought of Basil and his friends, the English rail buffs, and wondered what heights of ecstasy they would reach watching one of these black beasts plough through the snow in winter.

It was flat country, heading westward from Mudanjiang to Harbin, and every square centimetre of it was farmed. The train was travelling through the huge Manchurian Plain, China's largest wheat- and corn-producing area. In Siberia, there seemed to be vast tracts of arable land suitable for summer crops which remained untouched. But here, in the most populated country on earth, the land looked as used and worn as an old tyre. Not a single copse of forest stood, there were no birds, no wildlife. Shreds of tattered plastic blew over the furrowed soil, discarded after being used to keep the frost off last season's crops. Every kilometre or so there would be a small village, perhaps a dozen houses, perhaps a hundred. Twenty per cent of the world's population live in China, yet it only has seven per cent of the arable land. Still the country manages to feed itself.

I trundled off the train at Harbin Station and into the maelstrom of a large crowd. In the pushing and jostling throng, it struck me that the Chinese have a different sense of personal space to Westerners, but the crowd had a sense of humour rather than aggression. As soon as I stepped into the street I was greeted by what Harbin is most famous for: cold. Winter had ended, but a biting wind swept across the plains from Siberia in the north-west, slashing my face like a razor. It whipped up the dust and grit left

Above: *The north-east of China is a steam buff's dream. Many old locomotives still work the rails and up until only last year, China continued to manufacture engines at its factory in Datong. In 1987 China had an operating fleet of over seven thousand locomotives. This one, at the Harbin sidings, has a gold bust of a famous Communist General, Zhu De. The sign below says "Do the best for the Four Modernisations" and "Go forward before others".* **Left:** *Steam locomotives shunting at Harbin rail yards. While the government is slowly phasing out the use of steam passenger trains, steam is still widely used to pull freight, a practice which should continue well into the next century.*

In Harbin, the train drivers live in an age past. Faces black from shovelling coal, these drivers are on one of the many Chinese trains that still run on steam.

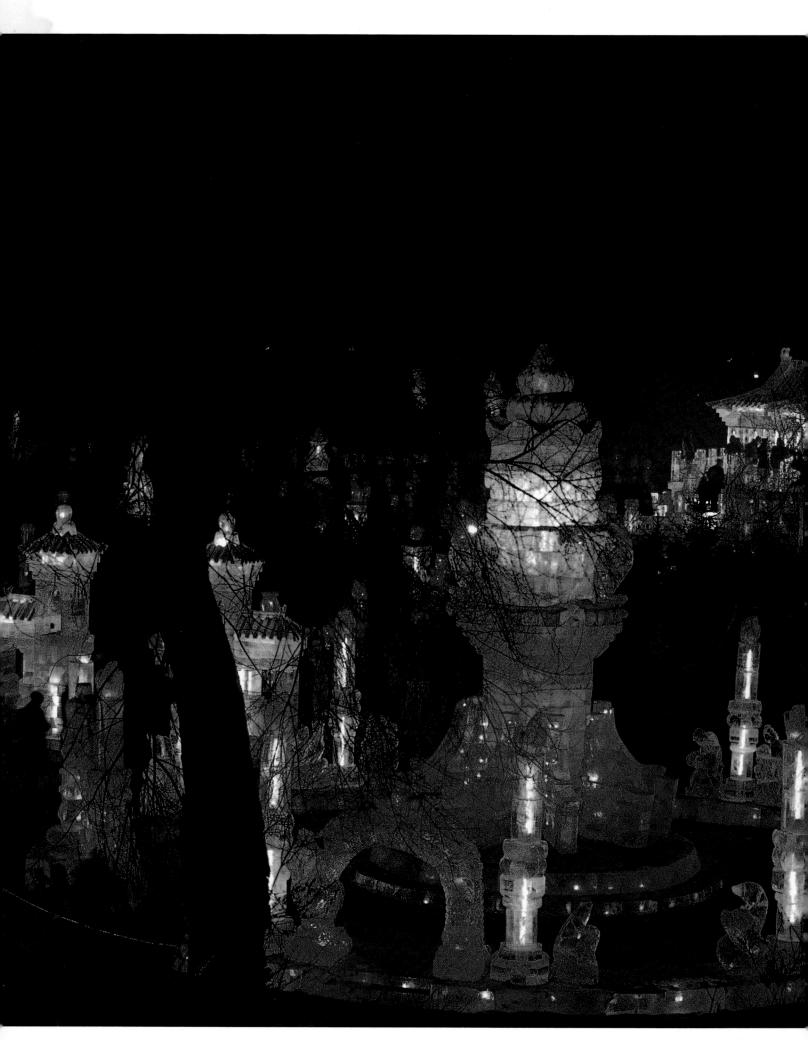

by the melted snow and within minutes I felt someone had emptied a vacuum cleaner in my mouth. I envied the women who wore thin scarves over their wincing faces to keep out the dust.

Harbin is the coldest provincial capital in China. In winter, temperatures can drop to minus thirty degrees Celsius or below. Summer is short and the region remains frozen for almost two hundred days of the year. It is a land of wind-chafed cheeks and runny noses, with the Chinese bundling up in fur hats with ear flaps, and so many layers of clothing that they look like Michelin tyre men. But despite the harsh conditions, I didn't find one local who wanted to live anywhere else.

"Heat makes you sleepy," one man told me. "In Harbin we are always alert."

Rather than being intimidated by the cold, the people of Harbin embrace it. The city has become well-known for its annual ice-festival, which rivals the winter festival held in Sapporo, Japan. On street corners and in Zhaolin, huge blocks of ice from the Songhua River are carved into sculptures of elephants, birds, bridges, planes and buildings. You can see miniature versions of the Taj Mahal, the Great Wall of China and the Eiffel Tower, all the more spectacular at night when a rainbow of lights frozen inside them is lit up. On the river, children play on giant ice slides, some people ice-sail and the most foolhardy swim in pools cut from the ice. The most absurd sight is of people eating ice-creams.

Harbin has an uncharacteristic history for a Chinese city. It is young, with a past dominated by foreign influence and control. Until a hundred years ago, what is now a city of over three million, was little more than a fishing village on the Songhua River. In 1896, the Russian Czar managed to extract permission from the corrupt Qing Dynasty to build a short-cut for the Trans-Siberian railway

With lights frozen inside the ice, the most spectacular feature of Harbin's annual ice festival is the ice sculptures at Zhaolin Park. Blocks of ice carved from the Songhua River are used to create over a thousand sculptures of famous Chinese temples and architecture. The first ice festival was held in 1983, and it now attracts over a million tourists a year.

Far left top: *The people of Harbin embrace the cold. Despite air temperatures as low as minus thirty degrees Celsius, Harbin's ice swimmers regularly plunge into a pool cut in the ice of the Songhua River. For the uninitiated, a quick dip could result in a heart attack. Warming up before entering the water is important.* Far left below: *An ice slide, built on the banks of the Songhua River, one of the amusements built for Harbiners to enjoy the cold winter.* Left top: *Couples travel from all over China to get married in a group wedding among the ice sculptures in Zhaolin Park, Harbin. Begun in 1984 with only two couples, it has grown in size every year to become a major event.* Left below: *As part of the ice festival activities, cultural performances are held in and around Harbin. They are usually variety performances with singing, dancing and comedy. Here an orchestra and choir perform for the people.*

221

through Manchuria to Vladivostok, establishing Harbin as a major railway junction and administrative centre. The Russians gained further control over the region in 1914 after the British, without consulting the Chinese, gave them full concessional rights to the land covered by the railway. Harbin became a cosmopolitan city and a major trading centre. Only nine days from Paris by rail, it could boast that it received the latest music, fashions and magazines days before Peking (Beijing) or Shanghai. Following the Russians, the Japanese stamped their presence on Harbin between 1932 and 1945, invading Manchuria as part of their dream of Asian domination, but the city's architecture reflects Russia's influence, not Japan's. With the occasional onion-domed church and squat office blocks painted in pastel colours like I'd seen in Leningrad, Harbin has a Russian feel. There is even a Russian restaurant in a rather pompous building in the old town centre which serves food more traditional than anything I'd seen in the Soviet Union.

But the thing that most struck me about Harbin was the sheer abundance of food and consumer goods. The free markets dotted around the city were piled high with meat, vegetables and fruit providing the colour Soviet streets lacked. You could walk into any state store and see shelves full of goods, such as cloth, toiletries, kitchenware. There were fridges, washing-machines, radios and radiators. The streets were full of advertising, the bane of the West, but at least a sign the economy was alive. For a humble visitor, the greatest pleasure was simply being able to walk into one of the city's many restaurants and order a decent meal without drama or fuss.

Despite problems with rampant inflation and growing unemployment, the relative prosperity China now experiences began with a series of economic reforms introduced in 1978 by

Left: *In a country long plagued by famine, there is no sight better than a shop full of food.* **Above:** *While the streets in Soviet cities are notable for their absence of food, in Harbin it is abundant. Here a night market stall sells fruit grown in the south of the country.*

Deng Xiaoping, the "capitalist roader" who re-emerged after the Cultural Revolution. Deng called his reforms the "second revolution" and "the new long march". In essence, the reforms were little different from those being introduced into the Soviet Union now. The command economy of centralised control was loosened, limited private enterprise and free markets were allowed and an "open door" policy to foreign investment was encouraged. With the Chinese acumen for business partly unleashed, the economy underwent a miraculous transformation, particularly in the area of agriculture. The irony of Deng's reforms is that they helped create the intractable tensions that now exist in China, encouraging the very liberalisation the government has suppressed.

Just to the north of Harbin I was introduced to a man who, the local authorities proudly boasted, symbolised the ability of socialism to work hand in glove with capitalism. His name was Shi Shanlin, and in a communist country he was a rare breed: a millionaire. I met him at his neat factory where he controls a multi-million dollar enterprise manufacturing water pumps. Designed by himself, the pumps sell throughout China and are exported to Japan and other Asian countries. A thousand people work at this factory, and it claims to make a net profit of over two million US dollars a year, all of which is ploughed back into the company.

A formal man in his mid-forties, Shi Shanlin spent ten years in jail for speaking out against the hard-line Maoist policies of the Gang of Four and the Cultural Revolution, China's dark decade when a million people were killed, and millions more repressed and starved at the hands of the reactionary Red Guards. It so perverted the natural order that parents were shamed, beaten and in some instances even killed by their own children. Twice Shi Shanlin had been sentenced to death but had the sentence commuted.

"Because of my objections to the Gang of Four, I spent a very difficult time in prison," he said. "I had to eat food that was inedible, live in a place that was uninhabitable and endure what was insufferable. I was right at the bottom of society."

Now, Shi Shanlin is hailed as a politically sound role-model for Chinese businessmen. Not your greedy capitalist, however, he claims to pay himself only a small wage and lives in a state provided house. For the Chinese government he represents a non-threatening image of entrepreneurial flair and socialist conscience.

"Financial return is not the reason why I am running this enterprise now," he told me. "Through establishing this business I am doing something in keeping with the reforms. If I am proved successful it will be an experience for others — if I fail then it will serve as a lesson to be learnt. All I require for myself is enough to wear and eat and it is okay. I feel that communism is for the benefit of all mankind, for the masses of workers, whereas capitalism is totally based on money, profit-making is above everything. We believe in friendship and compassion for each other. The people will fully enjoy the benefits of democracy and civil rights in the future."

I couldn't work out quite what I was listening to. It seemed like a lecture and I felt uncomfortable about the whole exercise. What bothered me most was that the Chinese were quite willing to parade examples of people who had supposedly bridged the gap between socialism and capitalism, but they had no interest in introducing me to those who saw irreconcilable differences.

My guide was a polite gentleman from the Cultural Bureau of Harbin who had remained quiet for most of the time.

Shi Shanlin at his factory. A millionaire in a communist country, he is hailed as a politically sound role-model for Chinese businessmen.

As we drove in his Mercedes back to the city, I discovered it was his duty to "review" all cultural activities in Harbin. Basically it meant he was in charge of all "culture". I asked what he censored or discouraged.

"Some people want to make films and write about liberty, but this is not what the government is trying to encourage," he said. "The government wants films about unity and about the good future of the people. But artists are not so keen to make films on airy fairy ideas like this, so they tend to make more love stories, Kung Fu films and such like."

"Is it okay to criticise the government?" I asked.

"There are forms of criticism which are okay, others that are not. It is not possible to go against Marxist principles, but it is okay to criticise corruption."

"What would happen if a writer came to you with a book calling for liberty and democracy in China?"

"I would advise the writer to change the book."

"If he didn't, would the book be published?"

"No."

I could smell coal and steam again as I briefly poked my head out the window of the overnight train which would take me through the famous Yellow Earth region of China and on to Beijing. For the moment we were still on the Manchurian Plain, and the land was much the same as I had seen earlier, kilometre after kilometre of ploughed fields waiting to be seeded for the spring. Thankfully the travelling distances were shorter here than Siberia, for the train was less than luxurious. I was travelling in "hard class", where each carriage consisted of a string of open-ended compartments with six bunks in each. There were no doors to close, so the whole journey became a very public affair. The Chinese had no qualms about

dropping rubbish onto the floor and it was soon littered with apple cores, chicken bones and peanut shells. The toilet was primitive; just a blunt hole in the floor which required a gymnast's balance to squat over. With no pipe or baffle, it emitted dangerous gusts of cold air — an unpleasant experience when the temperature hovers around freezing and the wind chill factor takes on a frightening dimension.

To very quickly see the class divisions in Chinese society I only had to walk into the "soft sleeper" carriage next along. With four bunks to a cabin, it was no more comfortable than second class on the Trans-Siberian, but in China it represented luxury and status. It was only half-full, mainly with army officers and party officials, who wore their little signs of privilege like badges of rank, good watches, rows of shiny pens in their breast pockets, quality briefcases. They seemed far removed from the cares of the many peasants jammed in "hard class" just a few metres away.

Late that night the train entered the cluttered outskirts of Changchun, five hours south of Harbin, and capital of Jilin Province. It is a busy industrial city of over a million people — China's Detroit — best known for its production of the Red Flag limousines used by senior party officials, and the Liberation truck, the ubiquitous workhorse that has barely changed in design since they were first assembled in the 1950s. When the Japanese occupied Manchuria from 1931 to 1945, Changchun served as military headquarters for the occupying forces and capital of the puppet state of Manchuko. Pu Yi was installed as the puppet emperor, but after the Japanese were defeated, he was jailed, finally ending his days as a gardener in Beijing. His last concubine, Li Yuqin, still lives in Changchun.

Fourteen million people were massacred by the Japanese during the

The last concubine, Li Yuqin, sits in the bedroom of her former husband, Pu Yi, the last Emperor of the Qing Dynasty. She married Pu Yi in 1943 and divorced him in 1957, only spending two years with him in Changchun during the time he was the Puppet Emperor of Manchuko (Japanese Manchuria).

occupation, but one of the least known, most brutal sagas was the experimentation camp they established on the outskirts of Harbin. Unit 731 was officially an "epidemic prevention and water supply unit", but its real task was to make biological weapons, in particular a "bacterial bomb" which could win the war for Japan. For guinea pigs they used Chinese, Russian, and Allied prisoners, conducting a methodical series of ghastly medical experiments. People were dissected without anaesthetics, injected with diseases like bubonic plague, anthrax, cholera and left to die. To conduct experiments on frostbite arms were frozen then fingers knocked off, some prisoners were boiled alive and electrocuted. Three thousand were killed, but no-one was brought to task during the Tokyo War Crimes tribunal. In well-documented evidence it was recently revealed that the Americans and British traded immunity from prosecution for data gathered by the unit.

The train was travelling through the Hebai Plain, bordering China's Yellow Earth Region. Bisected by the Yellow River, the soil the Yellow Earth region is famous for has come not from the water, but from the air. Over the centuries powder-fine earth and dust has blown down from the deserts of Mongolia, leaving a fertile loess which in some places is up to 100 metres deep. The region is the cradle of the Chinese civilisation and its soil has been cultivated for more than three thousand years. Little or nothing of the original forest remains.

Amongst the crowd in the dining-car I met a Chinese farmer in his early sixties who was making quick work of a bowl of noodles. A stocky man in a Mao jacket and cap, his name was Yang Zhonggui. Having visited relatives in the north, he was returning to his small farming village near Shanhaiguan, where the Great Wall

Above: *Boarding the train to Beijing. Pushing and shoving is commonplace in China, and queueing almost unheard of. Many people only have tickets for standing room on trains and are keen to be first to stake their claim to a space. If you don't fight too, you quickly get left behind.* **Right:** *No matter the weather, bicycles are the main form of transport for most Chinese, and continue to be the most efficient and cheapest.*

Life has never been better according to Mr Yang Zhonggui, a farmer near Shanhaiguan, to the east of Beijing. Agricultural reforms introduced ten years ago allow him to sell surplus produce on the free market and he now owns a tractor, fridge, colour television, washing machine and solar hot water system. Like many farmers (eighty per cent of the population) he is a strong supporter of the government. "The farmers are extremely happy, therefore we strongly object to the recent anti-revolution movement in Beijing. We were furious with the rebels, we wanted to rush to Beijing as soon as possible to eliminate that minor group of rascals."

of China meets the sea. He was travelling in the "soft seat" section of the train — hardly a poor peasant — and I discovered that he was the local *Cun Zhang*, or village head (which in effect made him the Communist Party representative). He was a friendly man, but talking to him was like listening to a tape recording.

"The villages are advancing in the direction of modern science," he recited, "Scientific management systems are used to increase production, therefore, the farmers have become rich. It is due to 'The People's Financial Improvement Policy' of the Party. We have clearly benefited, especially after the third section of the 11th National General Conference."

He was full of rote polemics and political slogans, singing the praises of the Party and Deng's "Four Modernisations". A simple man, there was no doubt his enthusiasm was genuine, indeed there are few in China who would disagree that the agricultural reforms introduced in 1978 have worked. The commune is dead, and while it is still impossible for farmers to own land, they are now able to contract it from the state which then buys a certain amount of produce at a fixed price. Any surplus can be sold at free markets where price is determined by supply and demand. Gloating about the success of the reforms, Mr Yang said that in the last three years he had added seven rooms to his house, bought a black and white television set — then replaced it with a colour one — bought a tape recorder, washing-machine, refrigerator, wardrobe, dressing-table unit, and even installed a solar hot-water system. Next he wanted to buy a video recorder.

"To be quite honest," he said, "We are not lacking anything else but this. Every family has enough clothing and food. Every family lives in big tall mansions."

Not every farmer is doing as well as

Mr Yang, but his relative wealth is symptomatic of growing divisions and inequity in Chinese society. While some farming families can earn an income equivalent to around $US6,000 a year, the average factory or office worker in the city has an average income of under $US250. Many urban dwellers feel a simmering resentment about the relative wealth of farmers, and say they are being denied the same opportunities and economic freedoms. While the government invests heavily in the countryside, the cities suffer a failing infrastructure, inadequate services and poor accommodation. Such tensions have been inflamed by allegations of government rorts and corruption. According to one unofficial estimate, some ten per cent of GNP is spent by millions of party bureaucrats on free meals. Rumours abound about party officials re-directing funds into their own businesses. These were amongst the reasons so many ordinary urban dwellers supported the 1989 student movement.

I asked Mr Yang what he thought about the student protests in Beijing.

"The farmers are extremely happy, therefore we object strongly to the recent anti-revolution rebel movement in Beijing. I could even say this, when many of us farmers heard about this kind of news, especially the older generation of farmers, we were furious with the rebels; we wanted to bite them, even to kill them. Nothing can reduce our hatred for them. Do you know why? It was not easy to make this nation. We have been liberated for forty years, the farmers have changed their social status, we are liberated and we have been given our rights. But the young people of this generation are trying to topple our Communist Party. We farmers will not allow that to happen."

"Where did you learn about the protests?" I asked.

"The news. We saw it on television.

A peasant woman and her daughter while away the hours in "hard sleeper". With the increased wealth in the countryside, more and more peasants can now afford the luxury of sleeping on overnight journeys rather than sitting or standing. Due to the high numbers of Chinese travelling, the government has recently raised the price of rail fares, in some cases doubling them, to try and stem overcrowding on the trains.

While many people in the West mourn the passing of the Steam Age, here it is very much alive. Steam locomotives are still more common than diesel or electric in China, especially in the north. This train is heading south to Beijing from Harbin.

They set fire to our military vehicles, they hurt our Liberation soldiers, and our Liberation soldiers were beaten to death. We were infuriated, we wanted to rush to Beijing as soon as possible to eliminate that minor group of rascals."

I asked whether he knew if any students were killed by the military.

"We didn't see that," he replied.

I shuddered to think that Mr Yang may represent the vast majority of farmers and peasants who make up eighty per cent of China's population, with three hundred million still illiterate. If he did, then the potential for change in China seemed bleak. Here was a simple man whose main struggle in life, like generations before him, was to provide food for himself and his family. In this he had succeeded and succeeded better than any generation before him. My own notions of democracy and freedom seemed a middle-class luxury when, for most Chinese, the notion of freedom means freedom from hunger. Why shouldn't he be supportive of a government which had delivered him relative prosperity? Why shouldn't he oppose a student minority who appeared to threaten it? Like many Chinese he had a Confucian belief in obedience and stability, and the need for a ruling class. To combine his zealous faith in the Party, with the Party's ability to control and distort information through the very television it helped him buy, seemed a potent mix. Blinkered by himself, blinkered by the Party, it was a vain hope to think reform would ever come from Mr Yang or his kind.

"In my opinion the focus of the Party should be in the area of reinforcing political philosophy," Mr Yang told me as we approached his station. "We should promote the heroes and heroic behaviour. This we have to carry out immediately."

As he walked off the train I imagined a gun in his strong farmer's hands, held at the head of a young student. I wondered if he was so convinced of his righteousness that he could pull the trigger and "eliminate the rascal".

The country heading towards Beijing was flat and unvaried. There were no trees, just clumps of houses between dull fields that seemed defeated by centuries of crops, of ploughing, of people. I came from a young country, where land was in some places still being cleared, and footsteps had never been felt. Here, it was as if every grain of soil had been whipped into place, too beaten even to support a renegade weed. Yet every spring it somehow kicked into life and sustained the masses, and would probably do so for another three thousand years. As I got closer to Beijing, untidy factories started to appear on the city's outskirts with a growing melee of cars, bicycles, advertising and people. Off in the distance I could see a thick forest of cranes, and an increasingly vertical city of flats, hotels and office buildings. I was acutely aware of crossing the border of two Chinas which symbolised the country's dichotomy. Behind me were the Mr Yangs, the peasants, the old mentality; ahead of me was an urban population of ten million people, full of "capitalist roaders" and "bourgeois liberals", who had tasted freedom and were struggling to escape the straightjacket that bound them. For the moment, the Mr Yangs had control.

The train slipped in under the enormous vault of Beijing Station, a colossus of a building and a relic of friendlier Sino-Soviet relations in the 1950s. The throng of people reminded me of the crowd at Yaroslavl Station in Moscow. It was the proletariat on pilgrimage — journeying to the capital with full bags and roped-up boxes — leaving with televisions, radios, fans and food. I was met by a smiling young woman from a guide service, who burst, unprompted, into an eager talk about the Beijing massacre.

For Chinese peasants, the horse and cart remain the main form of transport for heavy loads. Despite increased wealth in the countryside, cars and trucks remain concentrated in the cities or are for use only by factories or government organisations.

235

The Temple of Heaven is as much a part of the imperial splendour of Beijing as the Forbidden City. The Emperor would come here just before the winter solstice to pray for good harvests and protection for his subjects. Built according to ancient astronomical calculations, the temple symbolises the intricate balance between the heavens, earth and man.

Li Jianping, a young dancer from Beijing, expresses his ideas through dance.

In surroundings of traditional China (the Temple of Heaven), and temperatures of minus fifteen degrees Celsius, he performs a modern dance expressing his frustration at the present, and confusion as to the future, of China.

"You have heard about our troubles," she said, half-asking, half-telling me. "We believe many people were killed, but it is difficult to know how many. I was inside with my family and all I could hear were occasional shots. We don't see any of this on our TV or radio, we only hear on the foreign news. My friend: her husband went to the protests and he never came back. You have heard about all this? Many foreigners have heard."

It was as if, in the face of the barrage of lies and propaganda, she was trying to confirm in her own mind the truth of what had happened. Her face lit up when I told her I had heard much about the massacre. Was there still much tension in Beijing I asked?

"Oh yes," she said. "We are angry, we are very angry. But we are angry in our heads and in our hearts . . . we don't speak about this."

It was impossible to travel through Beijing without the events of June 1989 simmering in the back of my mind. As I set off along the Avenue of Eternal Peace towards Beijing's wounded heart, Tienanmen Square, the massacre took its place as the last in a long string of dramatic events in modern Chinese history. The Avenue of Eternal Peace, a broad tarmac of a road, had seen them all. In 1949, Mao faced the avenue from the steps of the Forbidden City and proclaimed the foundation of the republic. The same spot saw the beginning of the Great Leap Forward and then that great leap backward, the Cultural Revolution. In the avenue's ugliest icon, the Great Hall of the People, China's current emperor, Deng Xiaoping, captivated the world in 1978 by announcing his string of reforms. And to the avenue's west in 1978, "Democracy Wall" symbolised the beginning of a movement which, a decade later, saw the entire length of the Avenue of Eternal Peace become a road to democracy for hundreds of thousands of people.

Beijing's most imposing edifice, the Great Hall of the People (the seat of government), is now an ideological fortress against them. Standing beside Tienanmen Square, it was built with the help of Soviet engineers in the 1950s, a memorial to the birth of Chinese socialism.

Finally, it became a bloody dead end.

In the vast arid expanse of Tienanmen Square — the largest square in the world — the official face of order and respect had been firmly reimposed, but the scars were still obvious. The bullet holes and tank tracks were no longer to be seen, but tourists murmured quietly to each other as they peered at sinister stains on the ground. Edgy, po-faced security police were posted throughout the square, snapping and yelling at anyone who stepped out of bounds beyond a rope barrier. A bus backfired and people jumped. At the Monument to the People's Heroes, soldiers took photos of each other and as they pushed out their chests with pride, I couldn't help but think they were victory photos rather than happy snaps. Nearby, a hundred young schoolboys, all wearing red scarves of the Communist Young Pioneers, filed silently by on an excursion. They had been told about the counter-revolutionaries of 1989, but in ten years time would those same demonstrators become official heroes? (Students were brutally suppressed after a protest in 1976 following the death of Premier Zhou Enlai, but when the Gang of Four was deposed they suddenly became martyrs.)

On a subway wall under Tienanmen Square, a student wrote a poem, quickly removed, after the 1989 crackdown. "China, a father who's killed his son, is raping his daughter tonight. China, China, a living coffin. I've been buried in vain with you, for thousands of years."

In Moscow I had seen the body of the man whose ideology still permeated Soviet society, now I wanted to see Chairman Mao, the "Great Helmsman" who still ruled China from the grave. A giant photo of Mao hung from the Gate of Heavenly Peace at one end of the square, and at the other stood the enormous edifice of his mausoleum. It

At the monument to the People's Heroes, in the centre of Tienanmen Square, soldiers take snaps where the Goddess of Democracy once stood. There is no sign of dissent in Tienanmen Square now, just sinister stains on the pavement.

was probably ten times larger than Lenin's, only the Egyptians had built such absurdly big structures for the dead.

The queue was a strict line stretching five deep for 100 metres out into Tienanmen Square, but it moved at surprising speed. Up the steps and into the North Hall, we swept over crimson carpet past a giant marble statue of Mao as emperor, lording over China, and then into the Hall of Last Respects. Unlike Lenin's mausoleum, the whole room was harshly lit and with the distracting buzz of air-conditioning, it lacked the dignity and theatre of the former. Mao lay in a crystal coffin at the centre of the room, eyes closed, thin hair swept back from the high forehead. He had only been dead since 1976, but looked no more lifelike than Lenin who had died half a century before. His face had the same waxen sheen, his body the same eerie emptiness. History had disgraced Stalin. I wondered how this man would be regarded in fifty years time. Mao had given a humilated country its independence, a victory more for nationalism than communism, but he had also given the country the Cultural Revolution. "To put it bluntly," Mao once said, "It is (sometimes) necessary to bring about a brief reign of terror."

In the Chinese faces around me there was no trace of emotion, no-one looked anxious to stay, and as we jostled out of the room the whole ceremony seemed empty and heartless. But if there was any clue about where the real passions of the people lay, it was to be found seconds later when the throng spilt out the back of the mausoleum. It was like stepping from a church into a cheap sideshow. Suddenly I was in the midst of a consumer's carnival, a paddock of small stalls selling trinkets, toys, hats and clothes. Music thumped. Spruikers with loudspeakers hustled to sell plastic junk — small toy tanks of the PLO, battery-operated monkeys that did somersaults on the ground. I began to think these people had come, not to see the Great Helmsman, but to see the great sideshow. Despite its size and the man it contained, the huge temple of ideology behind them seemed irrelevant.

A little further down the Avenue of Eternal Peace I met another of China's dead heroes. Looking gallantly off into the distance, the noble face of Lei Feng towered above me on a billboard opposite the Military Museum of the People's Revolution. "Ideal, dedication, life," said the poster. "Emulate Lei Feng" and "Study Lei Feng thought". A humble truck driver in the People's Liberation Army, Lei Feng was canonised by Mao as the ideal communist man during the black days of the Cultural Revolution. According to the myth-making machine, Lei Feng was a selfless and conscientious soldier who spent his days doing good deeds and his nights reading Mao thought. He was the "Roger Ramjet" of Chinese communism, secretly washing his comrades clothes after work and giving all his savings to poor peasants. On railway trains, so the story goes, he not only gave up his seat to others, he even busied himself cleaning the windows and sweeping the floor. Until the Beijing massacre, however, Lei Feng had been all but forgotten. Now, his memory had been taken out of spiritual mothballs and re-enlisted in the fight against "bourgeois liberalism". All across the country he appears on posters, in shops, on trains. There is a television series about his life and a Lei Feng record distributed to schools with songs like: "We Want to Be Lei Feng Kind of Kids". At the military museum, a huge portrait of Lei Feng hung in the company of Marx, Lenin, Stalin and Mao. There was Lei Feng's diary ("I want to be a screw that never rusts and will glitter anywhere I am placed"), Lei Feng's socks, Lei Feng's gun and a plethora of stage-

Left above: A fashion parade in Beijing symbolises China's extraordinary contradictions. Economic reform and an open-door policy to the West have encouraged a wave of liberalism, Western ideas and fashions, the very things that now threaten the government. Left below: Lei Feng, the ideal communist man the people should emulate. He appears across China on posters, in shops and on trains.

Above: *With huge numbers of people wanting train tickets, and the backwardness of internal communications in China, buying a ticket is not easy. Often ticket sellers hold tickets for someone more important who might arrive at the last minute, or for friends and relatives — a small example of how petty corruption is stifling progression towards modernisation.* **Right:** *The last train ride of the whole journey. After travelling some 16,000 kilometres from the Berlin Wall, it's a short trip from Beijing to the Yanshan Mountains and the Great Wall of China.*

managed photos showing Lei Feng doing good deeds. It was such a fairytale story it made me wonder whether Lei Feng ever existed at all, and if perhaps he was invented to instil obedience and a spiritless conformity in the people. But the fact he died ingloriously under a fallen telegraph pole made me think he couldn't have been a complete fabrication.

I asked one young Beijing student what he learnt from Lei Feng. He grinned and said quietly, "Don't go near telegraph poles."

For the moment, the old guard with their tired old heroes and stale shibboleths were in control of China. Those that had risen up against them; the students, intellectuals, and thousands of workers who gambled their lives to support the democracy movement in 1989, had been quelled. According to Amnesty International over a thousand were killed, and tens of thousands are in jail in China's own "gulag archipeligo". But their numbers were not small: even the government acknowledges there were protests in eighty cities, reflecting a broad discontent which went far beyond undergraduate politics. Where once though, there had been an outpouring of self-expression, now there was silence. It was difficult to gauge people's feelings. I met a young Chinese painter at a party who said that life after the massacre was like a series of aftershocks after an earthquake.

"First there was great fear during the crackdown," he told me. "We didn't know how severe the repression would be, how many people would be killed. But two or three months after the massacre there was a wave of elation. We were happy just to know that we were alive."

Most protestors had resigned themselves to waiting for the old guard to die, for the octagenarian Deng to smoke his last cigarette. The only

organised resistance was in tiny groups, usually friends, who met fleetingly to discuss reform. Beijing University, where it all began, was a vision of conformity and obedience. But there were more subtle protests, not overtly political; small ripples of activity which rose, were quashed, then rose again in another form. The survivors first flocked to parties, then the government banned large gatherings without official permission. There was a wave of rock concerts, then the government saw them as a hotbed of bourgeois liberalism and their numbers were reduced. Stray posters were hung on walls, then torn down. The pot simmered, but the lid was tight. All the while, the contradictions in Beijing remained, even starker now. There was economic reform but no political reform. The city was awash with Western ideas, culture, fashion, but there was no Western freedom. Lei Feng was sent in to fight for young hearts and minds against the singer Tracey Chapman. It seemed Deng's reforms now conspired to overthrow him.

I boarded a train for the last leg of my journey, the two-hour trip from Beijing, north to Badaling and the Great Wall of China. The train was crowded with excited Chinese tourists making a pilgrimage to the Wall; children were perched on the edge of their seats eating melon seeds and pointing out of the windows, couples held each others hands looking dreamily into the distance. After half an hour the scrubby Yanshan Mountains sprang up out of the flatness, and as the train began to climb, the first small sections of the Wall came into view. Clinging to steep ridges and dipping into gullies, I was in awe, not only of the engineering, but of the amount of brute labour it took to heave the stones into place. This was once the northern border of China, and when the Wall was at its

The Great Wall, or the "10,000 li wall", is the symbol of China. The Chinese government has recently restored many sections of the Wall that have been destroyed over the years. In one celebrated instance, an army unit that tore down sections of the Wall to build their barracks, was sent back to rebuild it.

Above: *Despite the reverence the Chinese hold for the Great Wall, it is everyone's desire to be immortalised on it. Graffiti stretches for miles.* **Right:** *Teenagers playing on the Wall. It is probably the dream of every Chinese to visit the Great Wall. Winter is the most beautiful time to see the Wall and the absence of people adds to the beauty and feeling of solitude.*

most extensive, scholars estimate it stretched 10,000 kilometres from the Yalu River in the north east to Xinjiang in the north west. It was begun in 403 BC, but re-built and modified countless times later, and in its present form is a relic of the Ming Dynasty over six hundred years ago. The effort of its construction made the Trans-Siberian pale by comparison.

When the train reached Badaling I walked up through the avenue of stalls and shops, all selling identical souvenirs, to the Wall itself. It was a massive, snaking edifice, disappearing into the haze as if it stretched to infinity. What remained of the Berlin Wall was some 16,000 kilometres behind me, but before me now the Great Wall of China looked more brutish than ever, walling in the last kingdom of a moribund ideology. Mao once said "Only socialism can save China." Perhaps now, only China can save socialism.

I walked half-an-hour along the Wall's ramparts, jostling with tourists from all over the world. Finally I found a spot alone and reached into the bottom of my day-pack. I pulled out something I'd carried all the way from Berlin, a small chip of the Berlin Wall. I slipped it into a crack and left.

The Dragon's Head, where the Great Wall meets the sea at Shanhaiguan. More than ever, the Great Wall symbolises China's isolation from the rest of the world. Once it protected the Middle Kingdom, now it marks the boundary of the last kingdom of a dying ideology.

RAILWAY INFORMATION AND AUTHOR'S ACKNOWLEDGMENTS

East Germany

Route: Berlin/Leipzig
Distance: 180 kilometres
Route: Leipzig/Prague
Distance: 240 kilometres
Gauge: Standard 1,435mm
Engine type: Czech built CS Class
electric locomotive

Czechoslovakia

Route: Prague/Krakow
Distance: 460 kilometres
Gauge: Standard 1,435mm
Engine type: Czech built CS Class Type
82E electric locomotive

Poland

Route: Krakow/Warsaw
Distance: 297 kilometres
Route: Warsaw/Vilnius
Distance: 480 kilometres
Gauge: Standard 1,435mm
Engine type: Polish built electric EU07
and ET22 Class and Czech built electric
EPO5 Class

USSR

Route: Vilnius/Leningrad
Distance: 700 kilometres
Route: Leningrad/Moscow
Distance: 670 kilometres
Route: Moscow/Vladivostok
Distance: 9,297 kilometres
Gauge: Russian Standard gauge 1,520mm
Engine type: Electric VL60 and VL80
Class, and Czech built CS Class

China

Route: Suifenhe/Harbin
Distance: 390 kilometres
Route: Harbin/Beijing
Distance: 1,260 kilometres
Gauge: Standard 1,435 mm
Engine type: Chinese built steam QJ Class
for some sections in the far north, then BJ
class diesel for main southern routes.

Space forbids me to thank all the people who were instrumental in putting this book together. To those I have neglected to mention, including the many people who helped me on my journey, my sincere thanks. A special thank you, however, must go to the following. To the researchers: Heather Forbes, Irene Ulman and Paul Sanda. To my publisher, Kirsty Melville and my editor, Julia Cain. My deepest thanks go to Jenny.

PHOTOGRAPHER'S INFORMATION AND ACKNOWLEDGMENTS

The last thing, except of course, if you happen to be a photographer, you would want to lug over 15,000 km would be 40 kg of cameras, lenses, films and other fragile photographic pieces. But I did, from the summer fields of Poland to the frozen rivers of Northern China, through temperatures up to −35°C, and in and out of planes, trains, automobiles and foreign hotel rooms.

A photographer's working kit evolves through a series of circumstances, preferences and individual finances. Mine is a "Long March" outfit, with a distinct preference for agility, quality, versatility and reliability. (There are few camera surgeons in Siberia.)

I avoid equipment that draws excessive battery power or is

unnecessarily heavy or bulky. I use gear which packs easily, is interchangeable and is low on maintenance.

Without sounding like a camera company endorsement, my Nikon FM2 manual camera system served my purposes perfectly. I am sceptical about other automatic camera systems with irrelevant gizmos and flashing lights. There is only one light that the photographer really needs to understand.

Despite the cost and often tiring circumstances, I chose to carry at least seven lenses with me on location each day (I carried twelve in all). The average daily working kit included 20mm, 24mm, 35mm, 50mm, 105mm, 180mm and 300mm lenses, all tucked into a large waist bag, where convenience and comfort were best guaranteed.

My choice of film came down to the ever reliable Kodachrome 64, coupled with the new faster Kodachrome 200 emulsion, that proved ideal in the insipid winter light and for making those gritty Chinese steam trains look even grittier.

Over all the locations travelled for the Red Express, the most common technical question put to me has been: "What is it really like working in −30°C cold?" The following are some experiences:

• Battery failure in the extreme cold would send motordrives into slow motion and exposure meter lights would twinkle then fade like falling stars.
• Filters would contract so much from their threads that they would regularly fall from the front of the lens.
• The operator's breath would become encrusted like icicles onto the back of the camera as well as freezing across the viewfinder glass.
• Film leaders would snap and film changing was invariably painful and clumsy.
• Acute condensation could virtually flood an unprotected camera, if it was taken too rapidly from a cold to a warmer environment, i.e. indoors.

First and foremost I would like to acknowledge all those people whose faces appear on the pages of this book. As is usually the case, I have relied as much on the goodwill of strangers to make my pictures successful, as I have on my cameras and film. They are the lifeblood of my work and I thank them and hope I have recorded them fairly.

I am indebted to the directors of each of the film episodes. I would particularly like to thank Hugh Piper, the director of the Soviet episodes, John McLean, the series producer, Pieter De Vries, the series cinematographer, Andrew Birbara, Toivo Lember, Guntis Sics and Graham Wyse, and Mary-Joy Lu and the rest of the "Captured Live" production staff.

I would also like to thank Lindsey Merrison in West Berlin, Christo Bakalski of Film Contact Berlin and Heather Forbes (apprentice Provodnik) in Poland. In the USSR I would like to acknowledge two photographers, Valery Tyurin from the Tyumen Komsomolets Newspaper and Ildar Shagautddinov from the Tass agency in Khabarovsk. Appreciation also to our Russian interpreter, Irene Ulman and thanks to Andrei, Alexei and Sergei our Russian fixers. In Northern China, thanks to Madame Wang Xignan from Hellongjiang Radio.

On the home front I would like to thank my best friend Ann O'Sullivan for holding my life together back in Sydney, during my extended absences. I hope the Russian hat and wedding ring can partly display my gratitude. To my mother Fay, thanks on behalf of the crew for our Christmas puddings in −30°C and to my father Ray for the specialist cold weather wiring to my cameras.

Appreciation to Jack Jagtenberg for the design of the book and to Michael Cordell, the book's author. Thanks to Kirsty Melville and Julia Cain at Simon & Schuster.

Finally I'd like to thank all those fervent foreign taxi drivers, who despite the odds, did not succeed in running the Red Express off the road. It was indeed a blessing to arrive home safely.

253

INDEX

Captured Live Productions Pty Ltd would
like to thank the following organisations
for their assistance: Japan Airlines, Palace
Hotel Beijing, Simpsons Solicitors and
Wildlight Photo Agency.

Video

In Australia, the video, *Red Express,*
featuring the journey on the Trans-Siberian
Railway, is available from Hoyts-Polygram
Video.